TERRIFIC
T-Shirt Quilts

Turn Tees into Treasured Quilts

Compiled by Karen M. Burns

Martingale®
Create with Confidence

Terrific T-Shirt Quilts: Turn Tees into Treasured Quilts
© 2016 by Martingale & Company®

Martingale®
19021 120th Ave. NE, Ste. 102
Bothell, WA 98011-9511 USA
ShopMartingale.com

Printed in China
21 20 19 18 17 16   8 7 6 5 4 3 2 1

Library of Congress Cataloging-in-Publication Data
is available upon request.

ISBN: 978-1-60468-703-3

MISSION STATEMENT

We empower makers who use fabric and yarn to make life more enjoyable.

CREDITS

**PUBLISHER AND
CHIEF VISIONARY OFFICER**
Jennifer Erbe Keltner

CONTENT DIRECTOR
Karen Costello Soltys

DESIGN MANAGER
Adrienne Smitke

MANAGING EDITOR
Tina Cook

PRODUCTION MANAGER
Regina Girard

ACQUISITIONS EDITOR
Karen M. Burns

**COVER AND
INTERIOR DESIGNER**
Connor Chin

TECHNICAL EDITOR
Beese Enterprises, Inc.

PHOTOGRAPHER
Brent Kane

COPY EDITOR
Sheila Chapman Ryan

ILLUSTRATOR
Lisa Lauch

Contents

Introduction 4

Working with Knit Fabrics 5

Assembling the Quilt 8

The Projects

TOO PRECIOUS TO PITCH 12

CHECKMATE 15

CHILD'S PLAY 18

GOT SPIRIT? 21

GO ZAGS! 26

WINNING COMBINATION 33

CONGRATS, GRAD! 37

ROAD TRIP 45

TWEEN DREAMS 48

IN TUNE 53

About the Contributors 64

Introduction

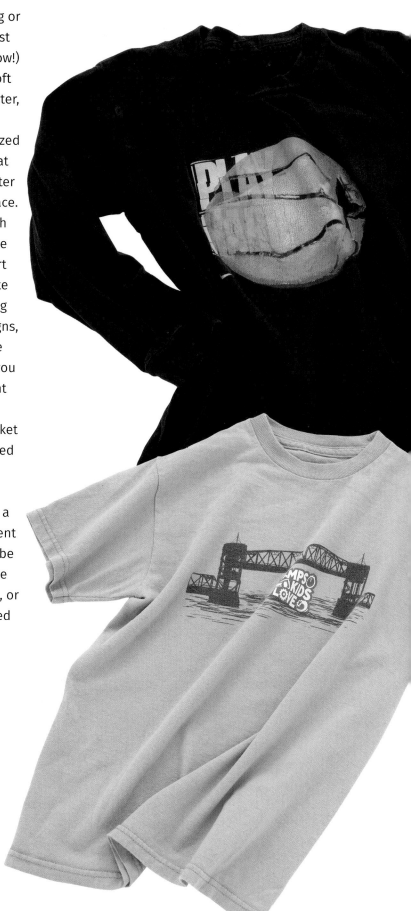

If you've got at least one kid in your life (young or old!), you've got T-shirts. And if you're like most quilters, at some point in your life (like right now!) you'll want to turn those beloved bundles of soft cotton knits into a quilt that your son or daughter, husband or friend will cherish.

But where to start? Working with different sized tees or motifs may seem troublesome. And what about stabilizing that knit fabric? What's a quilter to do? Don't worry, you've come to the right place.

We'll explain the ins and outs of working with knits, figuring out how to cut apart shirts for the best use of the fabric, and how to combine shirt parts with quilting cottons for sashing, alternate blocks, or borders. You'll even find tips for using mesh fabrics, screen-printed and iron-on designs, sweatshirts, baby clothes, and more. Plus we've packed into these pages 10 project ideas that you can use as is or modify to fit the shirts you want to use.

Has a T-shirt quilt been on your quilting bucket list for a while? Or have you just recently decided to make one secretly, to surprise a soon-to-be grad? Either way, you're about to become part of a wonderful club. As any quilter who's made a quilt from tees can attest, each time the recipient snuggles up in that one-of-a-kind quilt, they'll be reminded of favorite memories. Whether they're T-shirts bought on vacation, from sports teams, or band camp, you're about to turn those treasured tees into a warm and wonderful lasting hug.

Karen Costello Soltys
Content Director

Working with Knit Fabrics

The greatest challenge most quilters face when sewing with T-shirts is the stretch of the fabrics. The easiest way to deal with the stretch is to use a lightweight interfacing that will help control some of the stretch without making the fabric stiff and difficult to sew through.

HELPFUL TOOLS

Having the following items in your sewing stash will make constructing your quilt a breeze.

Interfacings. Before cutting patchwork pieces from T-shirts, stabilize the fabric with fusible knit or tricot interfacing. A lightweight knit interfacing won't add bulk but will prevent the T-shirts from stretching out of shape while you're cutting and sewing. Words to look for when choosing interfacing for T-shirt quilts are sheer, featherweight, lightweight, tricot, knit, and weft-insertion. The most common mistake quilters make is using a *heavy* interfacing, making T-shirt fabric difficult to piece and quilt and resulting in a finished quilt that feels like a piece of cardboard (not fun to sew or cuddle up with).

Choose a lightweight interfacing that will help stabilize the stretch of the T-shirt.

Rulers. A square acrylic ruler is a smart investment when making T-shirt quilts (not to mention other kinds of quilts). First, it will help you cut out the interfaced T-shirt squares. Second, a square ruler will help you square up pieced blocks. Even if you don't normally square up your blocks when piecing regular quilts, you may want to do so with T-shirt quilt blocks because, even though you've added stabilization with interfacing, the pieces have a tendency to "grow" while you're sewing. Consider finding a square ruler as large as (or larger than) the maximum size you anticipate cutting for your T-shirt quilt. Also look at rulers made for machine embroidery or those made specifically for T-shirt quilts. These usually have center lines or openings that help you easily center the logo or other design motif you want to feature.

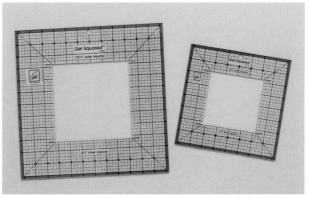

Acrylic rulers or templates, such as these Get Squared rulers from June Tailor (with 6½" and 4½" openings), are helpful when trimming T-shirt pieces to size.

Needles. For woven fabrics, you'll achieve best results using Sharp needles in your sewing machine. Ballpoint needles are recommended for sewing knits. Because these patterns combine wovens (quilting cottons) and knits (T-shirts), however, a universal needle is a good choice.

Pins. Flower-head pins, or those with larger heads (often sold as *quilting pins*), won't get "lost" as easily as regular pins in the bulk of T-shirt pieces you're sewing together.

Flower-head pins are easy to see, so you won't sew over them even with the bulk of T-shirt squares.

Rotary-cutting tools. Invest in a new rotary-cutter blade for no headaches when cutting through both T-shirts and lightweight interfacing.

STABILIZING A T-SHIRT

To prepare T-shirts for use in a quilt, you can either plan the quilt and cut out and interface only what you need, or "harvest" fabric from all your T-shirts first and see how much fabric you have to work with *before* choosing a quilt pattern. The basics for stabilizing follow, but also read "Tips for Fusing" on page 7 and "Handling Specialty Fabrics" on page 9 before fusing.

Approach 1: Apply Interfacing to Select Areas

First, plan which T-shirts you'll use for specific blocks. Then, cut interfacing pieces a few inches larger than needed for each T-shirt piece. This allows for shrinkage or shifting while fusing; once the T-shirt piece is interfaced, you'll cut it to the exact size. Just before cutting each T-shirt, turn it inside out and place the interfacing behind the logo area so that it ends up where you want it on the finished block.

Approach 2: Apply Interfacing to All Useable Areas

Interface *all* useable areas with a piece of interfacing that's a little smaller than the T-shirt area. Later, cut into the needed pieces for the quilt design you're making.

1 Cut the T-shirt up the sides and across the top to separate the front and back; remove the sleeves.

Using scissors or a rotary cutter, cut up the side of a T-shirt, close to the sleeve seam (so you can save the sleeve fabric, especially if it has a logo). Then cut across the shoulders and neckline, and down the other side.

2 Place the T-shirt front or back wrong side up on your work surface, and then place interfacing, fusible side down, over the desired area. (The fusible side is usually the bumpy side; when heated, the bumps become "glue" that holds the interfacing to the T-shirt.) Following the manufacturer's instructions, fuse in place and let cool. If you want to use the sleeves, cut off the underarm seam, open up the sleeve and interface. Be sure to put the stretch of the interfacing perpendicular to the greatest stretch of the T-shirt (usually the greatest stretch of the T-shirt will be around the body).

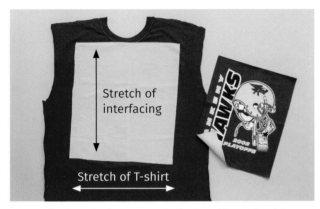

Cut the interfacing a couple inches bigger in either direction than the piece you plan to cut from the T-shirt. Fuse the interfacing in place, and then trim to the necessary size.

3 If the sleeves or hems of the shirts have ribbing (more likely on sweatshirts), cut this off before interfacing (it draws up the fabric) so you make sure you have a nice, flat piece to interface.

Often, T-shirts are knit in the round, which means they don't have any side seams. If you want to use longer strips of T-shirt fabric, cut off the body of the shirt so you have a tube, and then cut it into strips.

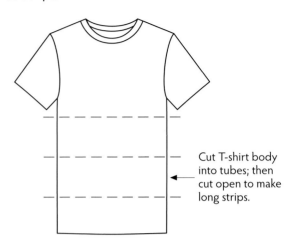

Cut T-shirt body into tubes; then cut open to make long strips.

TIPS FOR FUSING

When making a T-shirt quilt, you may actually spend more time pressing than you do sewing. Fusible interfacings are not all alike; if you purchase interfacing off the bolt, ask for the printed instructions (wrapped around the interfacing) when you have it cut. Some interfacings require steam and a lot of pressure; others require only a third the pressing time and require a particular iron setting.

Lower your ironing board so gravity can help do the work for you. Some fusibles require a lot of pressure for a good bond, and the lower the iron is (and the heavier the iron is), the less strain on your arms and back.

Once you interface T-shirt fabric, it will probably still have some give, but any wrinkles or wavy stripes you fuse into it probably won't stretch out, so make sure the stripes are straight and the fabric is flat on your ironing board before fusing.

Assembling the Quilt

Quilts in this book range from designs that use pieces all cut at one or two sizes to those that use a wide variety of sizes. T-shirt logos and motifs can be on the shirt's front, back, or both, and design size will vary widely, especially if you're using shirts acquired over a growing child's lifetime. The information below will help you plan a design based on the T-shirts you've collected.

CHOOSING A LAYOUT

If you're making a quilt that will incorporate T-shirt logos in a wide range of sizes, look for a quilt design that offers a variety of different shapes and sizes of T-shirt logo placement.

If the T-shirts you want to use are a wide variety of colors, consider a design that uses a sashing fabric to pull all the colors together. Sashing strips (sometimes alternating with sashing squares where blocks intersect) are strips that run between the quilt blocks. A multicolored print that combines all your T-shirt colors, or a solid color that looks good with every T-shirt, visually separates the blocks, and also unifies them.

Because T-shirt sizes and the motifs on them can vary widely, remember that you can add coping strips to enlarge blocks to a uniform size. *Coping strips* are strips of fabric added to one or more edges of a block or quilt section to make it large enough to fit adjoining blocks or borders. You can either make coping strips from the same/similar background fabric harvested from somewhere else in the T-shirt or add contrasting coping strips from a coordinating T-shirt or from quilting cotton (see "Winning Combination," below, for an example of the latter method).

"Winning Combination" (page 33) shows how to use assorted coping strips to make all T-shirt blocks the same size.

"Go Zags!" (page 26) is perfect for using both large and small logo pieces.

HANDLING SPECIALTY FABRICS

Often T-shirts, especially those from sports teams, contain tricky embellishments or fabrics that aren't quite conducive to typical quilting. If you've got any mesh, screen printing, or other fabrics you aren't sure how to handle, here are some tips for success.

Mesh or other fabric with open areas. Back the piece with coordinating fabric or contrasting fabric; baste the pieces together within the seam allowances, and then treat the pieces as one when constructing the quilt.

This rectangle, cut from a practice jersey made from burgundy-colored mesh fabric, is backed with an interfaced rectangle cut from a black T-shirt so it has a little bit of contrast without being jarring to the eye.

Screen-printed or iron-on designs. Some screen-printed designs can be ruined by an iron (or they can ruin your iron!), so play it safe and never touch the iron soleplate to the designs. Press from the back of the fabrics and/or use a press cloth or a scrap piece of fabric to protect the screen-printed area when you're ironing it.

Four-way stretch fabrics. For these fabrics, which are often used in dance or gymnastics costumes, try two layers of very lightweight tricot interfacing with the stretch of the interfacing layers going in opposite directions.

Embellishments on T-shirts. Embroidered areas on T-shirts can be difficult to sew through; try to center embroidered motifs in the middle of any pieces you cut for your quilt so you won't have to sew seams through the embroidery.

Sweatshirts or heavyweight fabrics, such as waffle weave. Use the lightest-weight interfacing you can to prevent even more bulk. Waffle-weave fabric tends to stretch even after it's interfaced, so you may need to trim it before *and* after sewing.

Kids' shirts, Onesies, and baby clothes. Look at the three quilts beginning on page 12. If you're combining clothes collected from throughout a growing child's lifetime, choose a quilt design that offers multiple-sized pieces so you have places to feature your (or their) favorite shirts. You could also sew together squares or rectangles cut from the smaller clothes until they equal the size of the pieces you're able to harvest from the larger clothes.

Too-small motifs/pieces. Besides the options listed above for kids' shirts, you could also cut out the motif or design on the T-shirt and sew it on top of a matching or contrasting background square; the background could be cut from another T-shirt or from quilting cotton. See "Checkmate" on page 15 for an example of this.

Non-ironable fabrics. Sew-in interfacings can be used to stabilize fabrics that should not be touched with the heat of an iron. Some dance costumes, T-shirts with glitter, and so on have metallic or other embellishments applied with heat; sew-in interfacings can help protect these fabrics.

Worn T-shirts or those with sheer areas. Consider using a lightweight fusible web (this is a paper-backed material that is used to "glue" two fabrics together) to fuse a white or other appropriately colored piece of fabric to the back of these T-shirts.

TIME TO SEW!

Sewing with knits is a bit different than sewing with woven cottons. Here are some tips you'll want to consider.

Seam allowances. Most quilts are constructed with ¼" seam allowances. But when sewing T-shirt quilts, some quilters, such as designer Mary Burns (see her "Congrats, Grad!" quilt on page 37), prefer ½" seam allowances. A wider seam allowance can help the seam allowances stay flat and not roll up. If you want to use ½" seam allowances on a quilt pattern that calls for ¼" seam allowances, you'll have to cut all of your pieces ½" bigger than the instructions indicate.

Stitch length. Because there's already more bulk in the seam when you're piecing with T-shirts, use a longer stitch length to avoid adding even more bulk and to avoid stretching the T-shirt fabric unnecessarily. A 3.0 millimeter length (as opposed to a 2.0 millimeter length) is a good length to start with. A very narrow zigzag stitch (1.0 millimeter width or less) can also help avoid the stretching that sometimes happens.

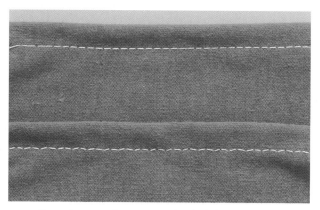

Use a longer-than-normal stitch length when sewing on knits *(top)*. A very narrow zigzag stitch can also help prevent stretch *(bottom)*.

Combining T-shirts with quilting cottons. Quilts can be made entirely from T-shirt fabrics, but to add more stability and decrease the weight of a T-shirt quilt, it's sometimes a good idea to add quilting cottons. These 100% cotton fabrics come in many designs at your local quilt shop or fabric store. They press crisply and have little bulk.

When joining T-shirt pieces and quilting cottons, always sew with the T-shirt knit on the bottom to avoid stretching the T-shirt. Quilting cottons often have more patterns and designs than T-shirts (which are often solid colored), so including them can add another design element.

Be sure to prewash the quilting cottons (even if you don't normally prewash your fabric). Because the T-shirts you're using for the quilt have most likely all been washed, if you don't prewash your quilting cottons, the finished quilt will shrink at uneven rates and will make the T-shirt areas puff out more than the cotton areas.

Walking foot. A walking foot is a sewing-machine attachment that helps both the top and bottom layers of fabric move more evenly under the feed dogs while you're piecing or quilting. It can help eliminate stretch in the top layer of fabric, especially when you're sewing two layers of T-shirt knit together.

A walking-foot attachment for your sewing machine will help prevent stretch when sewing layers of knit fabric together.

Handling bulk. Some of the tricks used when sewing denim can also help you sew knit fabrics. You can compress seams within the seam allowances with pliers and/or use a little gadget called the Hump Jumper, which lets you sew more easily over bulky areas. Stitch slowly over bulky seams, such as lapped openings of a polo neckline, embroidered motifs, and plastic zippers.

Pressing while piecing. As when interfacing the T-shirts, if there are screen-printed designs that might be heat-sensitive, press the seam allowances from the back of the piecing and/or use a press cloth.

Trimming after piecing. Even if you interface the fabric pieces, the interfacing usually doesn't take *all* the stretch out of the fabrics. Some pieces may "grow" more than others, so take the time to square up your blocks if you're sewing together pieces cut from T-shirts. For example, if you've sewn four squares together to make a Four Patch block, measure the block and compare it to what the quilt instructions tell you it should measure (including the seam allowances). If it's bigger than the desired size, trim it with an acrylic ruler and a rotary cutter.

FINISHING THE QUILT

Whether you're quilting it yourself or having it professionally quilted, there are some questions to answer before quilting. If your T-shirt pieces have any embellishments (embroidery, pockets, snaps, photos, etc.), decide how you want to treat those areas. If there are pockets on any blocks, do you want them sewn closed or left open? Do you want logos or photos stitched over, or would you rather have them only outlined with stitching? The quilts in this book have a variety of quilting treatments, so take a look and see which ones you prefer.

T-shirt pieces can be bulky where they're sewn together, so consider a loose allover quilting design, such as a loop or a stipple, which allows you to avoid the bulk of seam intersections. Other ideas include tying the quilt or stitching in straight lines through the centers of blocks (as opposed to stitching in the ditch between blocks).

If you're having your quilt professionally quilted, alert your quilter that it's a T-shirt quilt so that he or she's prepared. Answer the questions above and clearly communicate your preferences and expectations.

Too Precious to Pitch

Designed and made by Krista Moser
Quilt size: 38½" x 44½"

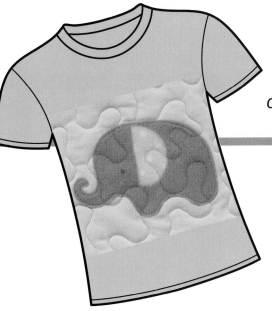

Do you have a stack of baby clothes full of memories that are simply too cute to toss? Why not keep them forever in a quilted display of those precious first years!

MATERIALS

Unless otherwise specified, yardage is based on 42"-wide fabric.

21 or more Onesies and toddler-sized T-shirts

¼ yard *each* of 8 assorted prints and solids for sashing

½ yard of multicolored print for binding

2½ yards of fabric for backing

45" x 51" piece of batting

3½ yards of 20"-wide lightweight fusible interfacing

CUTTING

From *each* of the solid and print fabrics, cut:

3 strips, 2½" x 42"; sort into 3 piles, 1 strip of each fabric per pile

From the multicolored print, cut:

5 strips, 2½" x 42"

PREPARING THE T-SHIRTS

1 Referring to "Stabilizing a T-Shirt" on page 6, prepare the printed front or back of each shirt or Onesie with interfacing.

2 Trim the prepared T-shirt pieces to the following sizes. On some of the squares and rectangles listed below, designer Krista Moser joined two to five T-shirt motifs to get pieces in the final sizes listed. She just made sure she cut them in sizes divisible by two plus ½" for seam

allowances so they would fit visually with the pieced sashing. For example, see the third vertical row of the quilt on page 12; three of the T-shirt pieces are cut 6½" wide but are made 8½" wide by adding an extra 2½" wide strip.

Note that the first measurement in each case is *width* because all of these are directional.

- 1 rectangle, 8½" x 10½"
- 1 square, 8½" x 8½"
- 1 rectangle, 6½" x 8½"
- 7 rectangles, 8½" x 6½"
- 8 squares, 6½" x 6½"
- 1 rectangle, 8½" x 4½"
- 1 rectangle, 6½" x 4½"
- 1 rectangle, 6½" x 2½"

Make It Your Own

TIP

If you're feeling adventurous, cut the blocks for this quilt to whatever size fits your shirts best. You just have to size them to numbers divisible by two plus ½" for seam allowance, such as 6½" x 8½", 12½" x 14½", or 2½" x 6½". These are all divisible by two and would fit together with the pieced sashing like a jigsaw puzzle.

MAKING THE BLOCKS

1 Sew together one pile of solid and print 2½" x 42" strips along the long edges to make a strip set. Press the seam allowances in one direction. Before sewing the remaining strip sets, double-check your ¼" seam allowances; the strip set should measure 16½" wide when finished.

2 Repeat step 1 to make a strip set from each pile of strips. Make them all the same color arrangement, or mix up the arrangement in each set for variety in the finished quilt.

3 Crosscut each strip set into 2½"-wide segments. You should get 15 or 16 segments from each strip set.

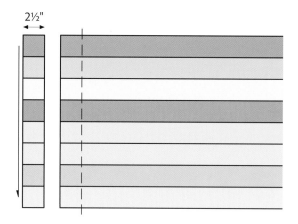

2½"

ASSEMBLING THE QUILT TOP

1 Referring to the layout diagram, arrange the T-shirt and Onesie squares and rectangles on a design wall in four vertical rows, leaving 2½" between them for sashing. Fill in the open areas between the squares and rectangles with the 2½"-wide pieced segments, unstitching between squares of the segments where you have too many. Make sure you like the arrangement of colors and that the sashing intersections don't have the same colors side by side.

2 Working on one vertical row at a time, sew together T-shirt pieces and 2½"-wide segments. Keep the T-shirt piece on the bottom toward the feed dogs with the segments on top; this will help eliminate stretching the shirts as you work. Press the seam allowances in one direction; work from the back of the fabric to avoid melting heat-sensitive designs on the shirts.

3 Join all vertical block and sashing rows to complete the quilt top. Press the seam allowances in one direction.

FINISHING THE QUILT

For free, detailed instructions on finishing and other quiltmaking techniques, refer to ShopMartingale.com/HowtoQuilt.

1 Layer the quilt top, batting, and backing; baste the layers together.

2 Quilt as desired. The featured quilt is stitched with an allover stipple.

3 Bind with the multicolored 2½"-wide strips. Add a label.

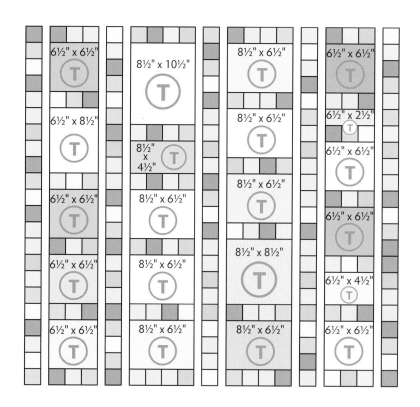

Checkmate

Designed and made by Jackie White
Quilt size: 52½" x 64½"

*T*wo colors of checkerboard borders surround T-shirt squares to make a pretty-in-pink throw. If the backgrounds of your tees aren't all one color, use Jackie's solution for appliquéing T-shirt motifs onto a coordinating background square.

MATERIALS

Unless otherwise specified, yardage is based on 42"-wide fabric.

20 child-sized T-shirts for blocks

1⅝ yards of pink solid for blocks, border, and binding

1⅝ yards of white solid for blocks

1 yard of green solid for blocks and border

3⅓ yards of fabric for backing

59" x 71" piece of batting

2¾ yards of 20"-wide lightweight fusible interfacing

CUTTING

From the pink solid, cut:
20 strips, 2½" x 42"

From the white solid, cut:
20 strips, 2½" x 42"

From the green solid, cut:
13 strips, 2½" x 42"

PREPARING THE T-SHIRTS

1 Referring to "Stabilizing a T-Shirt" on page 6, prepare the printed front or back of each shirt with interfacing.

2 Trim the prepared T-shirt pieces to 20 squares, 8½" x 8½". Designer Jackie White cut out some smaller T-shirt motifs with about a ½" border of T-shirt fabric, topstitched the motifs to another T-shirt back about ¼" from the edges, and then cut the necessary 8½" square.

MAKING THE BLOCKS

1 Alternating colors, sew together two pink and two white strips along the long edges to make strip set A. Press the seam allowances toward the pink strips. Repeat to make two strip sets. Cut the strip sets into 20 A segments, each 2½" wide.

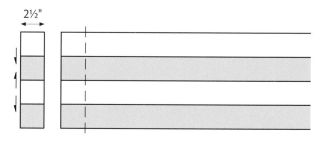

Strip set A.
Make 2, cut 20 segments total.

2 Alternating colors, sew together three pink and three white strips along the long edges to make strip set B. Press the seam allowances toward the pink strips. Repeat to make two strip sets. Cut the strip sets into 20 B segments, each 2½" wide.

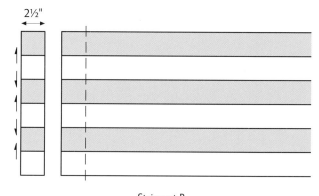

Strip set B.
Make 2, cut 20 segments total.

3 Repeat steps 1 and 2 using green and white strips.

4 Sew pink A segments to the top and bottom edges of a T-shirt square; rotate the A segment on the bottom so pink is on the left. Press the seam allowances toward the A segments. Add pink B segments to the remaining edges of the square to make a pink block; rotate the B segment on the right so white is at the top. Press the seam allowances toward the center square. The block should measure 12½" square. Make 10 pink blocks total.

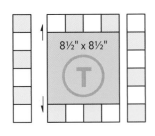
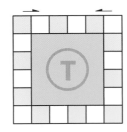

Make 10.

5 Using green A and B segments, repeat step 4 to make 10 green blocks, but press the seam allowances in the opposite direction from the pink blocks.

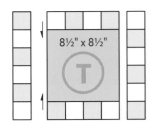
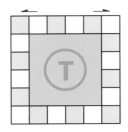

Make 10.

ASSEMBLING THE QUILT TOP

1 Referring to the quilt layout diagram above right and alternating block colors, lay out pink and green blocks in five rows of four blocks each. Join the blocks in each row. Press the seam allowances toward the green blocks. Join the rows and press the seam allowances in one direction. The quilt should measure 48½" x 60½".

2 Sew together three of the remaining pink strips end-to-end to make one long strip. Cut one 2½" x 48½" border and one 2½" x 64½" border from the long strip. Repeat with the three remaining green strips. Sew the short pink border to the top edge of the quilt and the short green border to the bottom edge of the quilt. Sew the long green border to the left edge of the quilt and the long pink border to the right edge of the quilt. Press the seam allowances toward the borders.

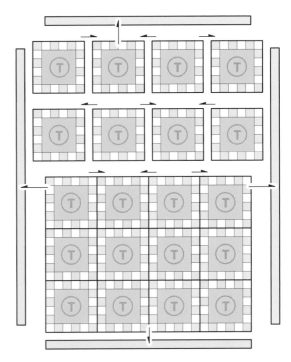

FINISHING THE QUILT

For free, detailed instructions on finishing and other quiltmaking techniques, refer to ShopMartingale.com/HowtoQuilt.

1 Layer the quilt top, batting, and backing; baste the layers together.

2 Quilt as desired. The featured quilt is machine quilted with a feathered vine in the checkerboard section of each block and in the border. Straight stitching highlights certain areas of each T-shirt design.

3 Bind with the remaining pink strips.

Child's Play

Designed and made by Elizabeth Tisinger Beese
Quilt size: 60½" x 60½"

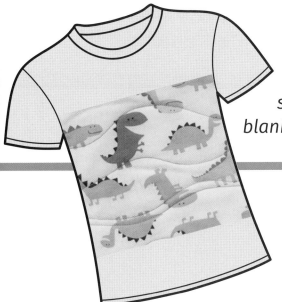

*T*ransform memorable clothing into something you and your kids can cuddle up with! Add happy polka-dot strips Log Cabin–style to squares cut from Onesies, T-shirts, receiving blankets, baby bibs, and swaddling sleepers.

MATERIALS

Unless otherwise specified, yardage is based on 42"-wide fabric.

18 to 36 Onesies and toddler-sized T-shirts for block centers (number of Onesies or shirts needed depends on whether you're using the fronts *and* backs of the shirts or just the fronts)

3⅜ yards total OR 18 pieces, ¼ yard each, of assorted polka dots for block borders

⅝ yard of multicolored dot for binding

3¾ yards of fabric for backing

67" x 67" piece of batting

4½ yards of 20"-wide lightweight fusible interfacing; Elizabeth prefers Pellon SK135 Sheer-Knit or Pellon EK130 Easy Knit

CUTTING

From the assorted polka dots, cut *18 matching sets* of:

2 rectangles, 3½" x 10½" (36 total)
2 rectangles, 3½" x 4½" (36 total)

From the remaining assorted polka dots, cut *18 matching sets* of:

2 rectangles, 2½" x 10½" (36 total)
2 rectangles, 2½" x 6½" (36 total)

From the multicolored dot, cut:

7 strips, 2½" x 42"

PREPARING THE CLOTHING

1 Referring to "Stabilizing a T-Shirt" on page 6, prepare the printed front or back of each shirt or Onesie with interfacing. If you're also using receiving blankets and sleepers, prepare them the same way if they are made of knit fabric.

2 Plan your cutting before starting. Keep in mind that most Onesies can be trimmed to make a 6½" square, but the design motifs often fit better into a 4½" square. If you'll be cutting overlapped clothing areas that have snaps or zippers, plan the cuts so that you avoid having snaps (or a zipper pull) within ½" of the edges of the square. Baste the openings closed at the edges of the square before or after interfacing.

3 Trim the prepared T-shirt pieces to make the following:

- 18 squares, 6½" x 6½"
- 18 squares, 4½" x 4½"

What about stains?

TIP

It's inevitable that some baby clothes will have stains, even if they're repeatedly laundered. If you don't think this adds to the charm of the quilt, you can often use the upper back of Onesies (the least likely place for spills). For embroidered or appliquéd motifs on a stained background, cut out the motif ⅛" or ¼" from the edge, center it on a background square cut from another T-shirt or from quilting cotton, and machine-stitch in place close to the embroidery or appliqué edge.

MAKING THE BLOCKS

1 For one A block, gather one T-shirt 6½" square for the block center and a set of matching polka-dot pieces (two 2½" x 10½" rectangles and two 2½" x 6½" rectangles). Sew the 2½" x 6½" rectangles to opposite edges of T-shirt square. Add the 2½" x 10½" rectangles to the remaining edges to make block A. Press all of the seam allowances toward the polka-dot pieces. The block should measure 10½" square. Repeat to make 18 A blocks.

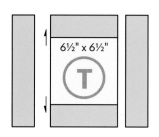
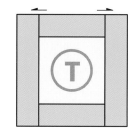

6½" x 6½"

Block A

2 For one B block, gather one T-shirt 4½" square for the block center and a set of matching polka-dot pieces (two 3½" x 10½" rectangles and two 3½" x 4½" rectangles). Sew the 3½" x 4½" rectangles to opposite edges of T-shirt square. Add the 3½" x 10½" rectangles to the remaining edges to make block B. Press all of the seam allowances toward the polka-dot pieces. The block should measure 10½" square. Repeat to make 18 B blocks.

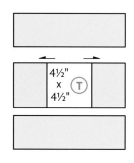
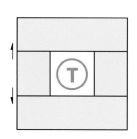

4½" x 4½"

Block B

ASSEMBLING THE QUILT TOP

1 Alternating A and B blocks and referring to the quilt layout diagram below, lay out the blocks in six rows of six blocks each. Try to distribute block colors and values evenly throughout the quilt. In the featured quilt, all of the blocks that have a directional block center face the same direction.

2 Sew together the blocks in each row. Press the seam allowances toward the B blocks. Join the rows and press the seam allowances in one direction to complete the quilt top.

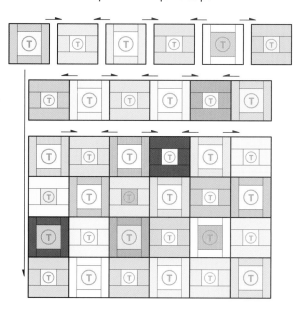

FINISHING THE QUILT

For free, detailed instructions on finishing and other quiltmaking techniques, refer to ShopMartingale.com/HowtoQuilt.

1 Layer the quilt top, batting, and backing; baste the layers together.

2 Quilt as desired. Elizabeth machine quilted random wavy lines horizontally across the quilt, avoiding stitching over heavily embroidered areas, snaps, or buttons. She stitched in the ditch vertically between block rows.

3 Bind with the multicolored 2½"-wide strips.

Got Spirit?

Designed and made by Penny Barnes
Quilt size: 56½" x 84½"

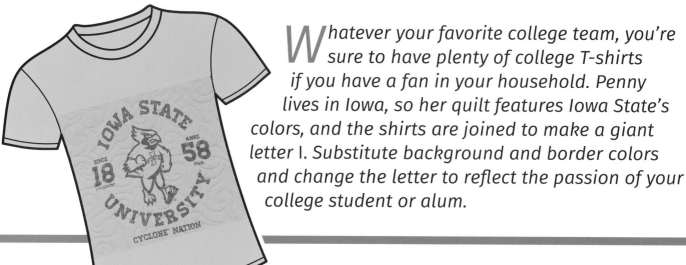

*W*hatever your favorite college team, you're sure to have plenty of college T-shirts if you have a fan in your household. Penny lives in Iowa, so her quilt features Iowa State's colors, and the shirts are joined to make a giant letter I. Substitute background and border colors and change the letter to reflect the passion of your college student or alum.

MATERIALS

Unless otherwise specified, yardage is based on 42"-wide fabric. The following fabric requirements are what Penny used to make this quilt. If you want to use a different letter (see other possibilities in "Team Options" on page 24), you may need a different number of T-shirts and different yardage for the frames and background.

9 adult-sized T-shirts

1¼ yards of yellow solid for background*

1⅛ yards of gray check for outer border

⅞ yard of black solid for block frames

⅝ yard of red print for inner border

⅝ yard of red-and-yellow print for binding

5¼ yards of fabric for backing

65" x 93" piece of batting

4⅛ yards of 20"-wide lightweight fusible interfacing; Penny prefers Pellon Sheerweight Interfacing 905F

*If your background fabric is wide enough to cut 40½" strips, you'll only need 1 yard of fabric.

CUTTING

If you want to use a different letter, refer to "Team Options" on page 24 for the number of T-shirt squares, black-solid strips, and yellow-solid background pieces to cut.

From the black solid, cut:
4 strips, 2½" x 42"; piece and trim to make 2 strips, 2½" x 72½"
4 strips, 2½" x 16½"
14 strips, 2½" x 12½"

From the yellow solid, cut:
2 rectangles, 14½" x 40½"

From the red print, cut:
7 strips, 2½" x 42"

From the gray check, cut:
8 strips, 4½" x 42"

From the red-and-yellow print, cut:
8 strips, 2½" x 42"

PREPARING THE T-SHIRTS

1 Referring to "Stabilizing a T-Shirt" on page 6, prepare the printed front or back of each shirt with interfacing.

2 Trim the prepared T-shirt pieces to nine squares, 12½" x 12½".

ASSEMBLING THE QUILT TOP

Refer to the quilt assembly diagram below as needed.

1 Lay out the T-shirt squares and black solid strips in five vertical rows as shown. First, join the black 2½" x 12½" strips to tops and bottoms of all of the T-shirt squares; press the seam allowances toward the black strips. Then add the black 2½" x 16½" strips to the left or right side of four of the T-shirt squares; press as before. Finally, sew the T-shirt squares, yellow 14½" x 40½" background rectangles, and black 2½" x 72" strips together. Press the seam allowances toward the long black strips.

2 Sew the red strips together end-to-end to make one long strip. Cut two 2½" x 72½" inner borders and two 2½" x 48½" inner borders. Sew the long inner borders to the long edges of the quilt and the short inner borders to the remaining edges of the quilt. Press the seam allowances toward the borders.

3 Sew the gray strips together end-to-end to make one long strip. Cut two 4½" x 76½" outer borders and two 4½" x 56½" outer borders. Sew the long outer borders to the long edges of the quilt and the short outer borders to the remaining edges of the quilt. Press the seam allowances toward the outer borders.

FINISHING THE QUILT

For free, detailed instructions on finishing and other quiltmaking techniques, refer to ShopMartingale.com/HowtoQuilt.

1 Layer the quilt top, batting, and backing; baste the layers together.

2 Quilt as desired. Penny machine-quilted a spiral-and-flame design in most of the quilt. In the yellow background, she drew the letters ISU with a washable marking pen, then stitched heavily around the letters to give them a raised, trapunto effect.

3 Bind with the red-and-yellow 2½"-wide strips.

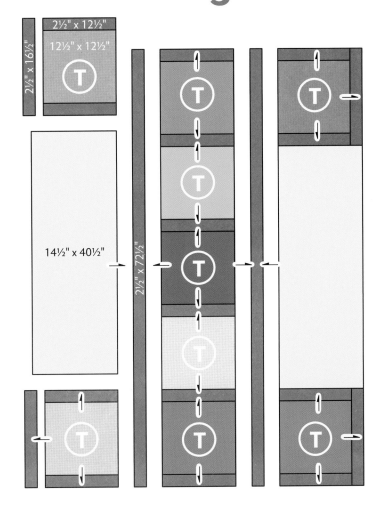

Team Options

Not all schools start with the letter I! If you'd like a quilt pattern that features a different letter in the design, these illustrations will show you the number of T-shirt squares, black solid strips, and yellow solid background pieces to cut. You'll notice that only some letters of the alphabet are included. That's because we included only those that can be made in a three-block-wide grid—the same layout as the "Team Spirit" quilt—without looking awkwardly pixelated.

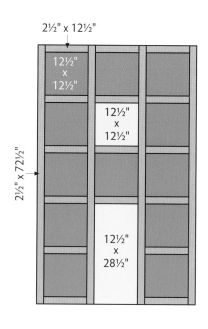

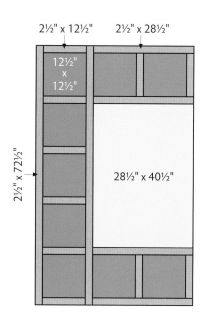

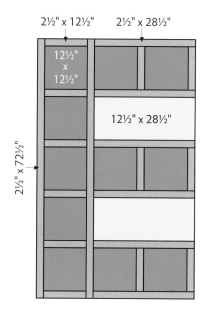

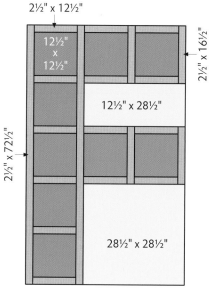

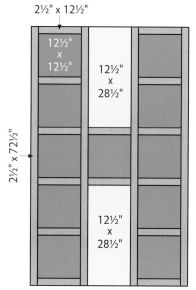

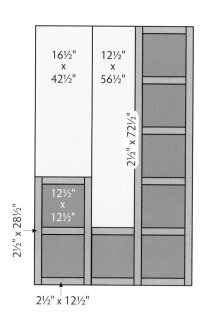

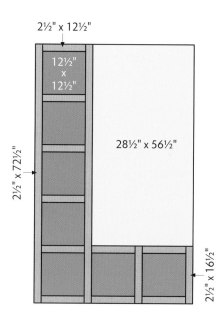

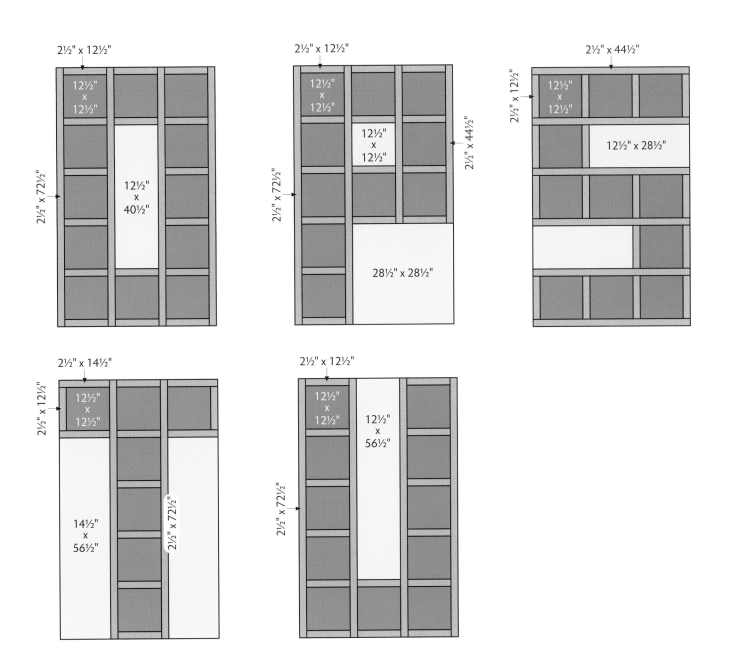

2½" x 12½"

12½"
x
12½"

2½" x 72½"

12½"
x
40½"

2½" x 12½"

12½"
x
12½"

2½" x 72½"

2½" x 44½"

12½"
x
12½"

28½" x 28½"

2½" x 44½"

2½" x 12½"

12½"
x
12½"

12½" x 28½"

2½" x 14½"

2½" x 12½"

12½"
x
12½"

14½"
x
56½"

2½" x 72½"

2½" x 12½"

12½"
x
12½"

12½"
x
56½"

2½" x 72½"

Go Zags!

Designed and made by Janet Nesbitt
Quilt size: 69½" x 78½"

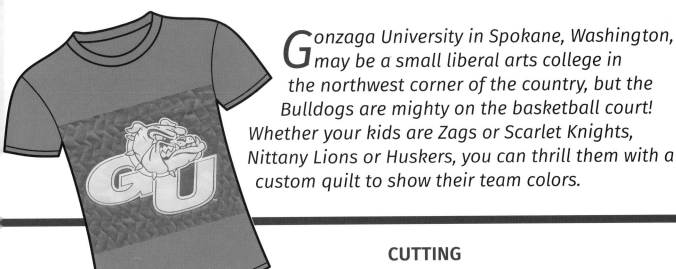

Gonzaga University in Spokane, Washington, may be a small liberal arts college in the northwest corner of the country, but the Bulldogs are mighty on the basketball court! Whether your kids are Zags or Scarlet Knights, Nittany Lions or Huskers, you can thrill them with a custom quilt to show their team colors.

MATERIALS

Unless otherwise specified, yardage is based on 42"-wide fabric. Fat eighths are 9" x 21".

Approximately 21 T-shirts in 4 or 5 colors (red, white, navy and/or black, and gray) for rectangles, squares, and border*

Fat eighths or scraps of 3 red prints, 1 cream print, 1 white print, 1 gray stripe, and 1 blue print for the shoe appliqués (7 total)

⅝ yard of dark-gray solid for binding

4¾ yards of fabric for backing

76" x 85" piece of batting

Approximately 8 yards of 20"-wide lightweight fusible interfacing

Template plastic

1 pair of children's shoelaces

1 pair of adult tall tube socks

*If you have some shirts that are printed front and back, you may need fewer shirts. A commemorative game towel is used in place of one shirt in the quilt shown. See "Cutting" at right for assistance with selecting your T-shirts with regard to color and motif size.

PREPARING THE T-SHIRTS

Before cutting, prepare the T-shirts. Referring to "Stabilizing a T-Shirt" on page 6, prepare the front and back of each shirt with interfacing.

CUTTING

From the prepared T-shirts, first cut the large squares and rectangles from the printed areas of the shirts, and then cut the smaller pieces and border squares from the sides, back, or even the sleeves of the shirts. The first measurement of each piece listed below is width because all of these are directional.

The appliqué patterns for pieces A–N are on pages 31 and 32. To use needle-turn appliqué, trace each pattern onto template plastic and cut out the template on the drawn line. Trace each template, right side up, on the indicated fabric. Cut out the fabric shapes, leaving a ¼" seam allowance. For free instructions on appliqué, visit ShopMartingale.com/HowtoQuilt. Stitch the appliqués by hand, sweeping under each edge with your needle as you sew.

From the red T-shirts, cut motif areas:

   A: 15½" x 15½" square

   B: 3½" x 6½" filler rectangle

   C: 3½" x 9½" filler rectangle

   D: 12½" x 12½" square

   E: 15½" x 6½" rectangle

   F: 3½" x 12½" filler rectangle

   G: 15½" x 21½" rectangle

   H: 12½" x 12½" square

   I: 15½" x 12½" rectangle

From the remaining red T-shirt pieces, cut:

18 squares, 6½" x 6½"

From the white T-shirts, cut:

   J: 12½" x 12½" square

Continued on page 28

Continued from page 27

    K: 3½" x 6½" filler rectangle

    L: 6½" x 9½" rectangle

    M: 15½" x 12½" rectangle

    N: 12½" x 15½" rectangle

    O: 15½" x 9½" rectangle

    P: 3½" x 12½" filler rectangle

    Q: 12½" x 9½" rectangle

    R: 12½" x 12½" square

From the remaining white T-shirt pieces, cut:
12 squares, 2" x 2"
12 rectangles, 2" x 3½"

From the navy and/or black T-shirts, cut:

    S: 9½" x 18½" rectangle

    T: 12½" x 12½" square

    U: 12½" x 15½" rectangle

    V: 15½" x 18½" rectangle

    W: 15½" x 15½" square

    X: 15½" x 27½" rectangle*

From the remaining navy and/or black T-shirt pieces, cut:
17 squares, 6½" x 6½"
1 rectangle, 3½" x 6½"
24 squares, 2" x 2"

From the gray T-shirts, cut:

    Y: 18½" x 18½" square

    Z: 3½" x 12½" filler rectangle

    AA: 12½" x 6½" rectangle

From the remaining gray T-shirt pieces, cut:
3 autograph squares, 3½" x 3½"**

Complete the shoe appliqué prior to cutting out rectangle X. If you're having trouble finding a T-shirt with enough height for this piece, it's fun to stitch a contrasting color (designer Janet Nesbitt just used white) underneath the collar of the shirt prior to adding the fusible interfacing.

**These are cut from T-shirts that have been autographed by players, with the signature centered in the square. If you don't have any autographed T-shirts, you can use solid squares, or fussy-cut a motif that you'd like to feature.*

From 1 red print, cut:
1 *each* of appliqué shapes A and G

From the 2nd red print, cut:
1 of appliqué shape D

From the 3rd red print, cut:
1 of appliqué shape K

From the cream print, cut:
1 *each* of appliqué shapes B, C, H, and J

From the white print, cut:
1 *each* of appliqué shapes F and L

From the gray stripe, cut:
1 of appliqué shape M

From the blue print, cut:
1 *each* of appliqué shapes E and I

From the dark-gray solid, cut:
8 strips, 2½" x 42"

MAKING THE BLOCKS

1 Using your favorite method of appliqué and referring to the diagram, stitch the two shoes to the X rectangle, leaving openings for the shoelaces where indicated on the patterns. (Janet used needle-turn appliqué, so the patterns are not reversed. If you want to use fusible appliqué, you'll need to reverse the patterns.) Cut each shoelace in half. Secure each of the cut ends beneath the appliqué. Trim the T-shirt to measure 15½" x 27½" (if needed) for block X.

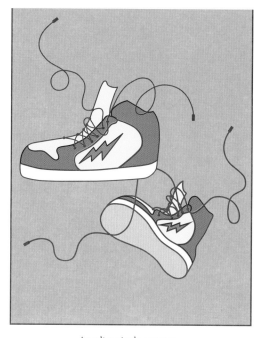

Appliqué placement

2 Cross the laces and hand stitch them in place for the first two lace holes. Then gradually add slack to the laces, tacking them in place with a few stitches. At the top of each shoe, refer to the photo as you continue stitching each lace to the background, leaving the loops and lace ends free and dimensional.

3 Place a navy T-shirt 2" square on one end of a white T-shirt 2" x 3½" rectangle. Stitch diagonally from corner to corner on the navy square. Trim the seam allowance to ¼" and press the seam allowances toward the navy. Repeat at the remaining end of the white rectangle to make a star-point unit. Make 12 star-point units.

Make 12.

4 Sew together four star-point units, four white T-shirt 2" squares, and a gray T-shirt autograph 3½" square in three rows. Press the seam allowances away from the star-point units. Join rows to make a border Star block. Press the seam allowances in one direction. The block should measure 6" square. Make three border Star blocks.

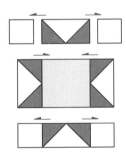 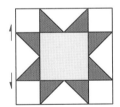

Make 3.

ASSEMBLING THE QUILT TOP

1 In preparation for constructing the quilt top, join the following pieces while referring to the quilt layout diagram on page 30. Press all seam allowances in one direction.

- Sew a red 6½" square and the B rectangle together; sew this unit to the S rectangle.
- Sew four navy and four red 6½" squares together to make the left border. Repeat to make the top border.
- Sew the J square to the T square.
- Sew the N rectangle to the Z rectangle.
- Sew the F, AA, and Q rectangles together; sew this unit to the V rectangle.
- Sew the R square and I rectangle together.
- Sew the H square and P rectangle together. Sew the O rectangle and the W square to this unit.
- Sew the M, G, and X rectangles together.
- Sew five navy and five red 6½" squares together to make the right border. Sew the right border to the M/G/X section.
- Sew four navy 6½" squares, four red 6½" squares, the navy 3½" x 6½" rectangle, and three star blocks together to make the bottom border.

2 Construct the quilt in sections in the order below. Some pieces and sections are joined with a partial seam as shown in the quilt layout diagram. Sew only the distance indicated by the ⊢—⊣ icon. Complete the seam when instructed to do so.

- Sew the U rectangle to the K rectangle with a partial seam.
- Sew the Y square to right edge of the unit.
- Sew the J/T unit to the top of the unit.
- Sew the A square to the left edge of the unit.
- Sew the E rectangle to the O/H/P/W unit with a partial seam.
- Sew the unit to the bottom of unit U/Y.
- Sew the C rectangle to unit N/Z with a partial seam.
- Sew the C/N/Z unit to the left edge of the U/E unit.
- Sew the C/U unit to the A/K unit, completing the seam between K and U.

- Sew the V/F/AA/Q unit to the R/I unit. Sew this section to the edge of the Z/E unit.
- Sew the E/F/AA/Q/I unit to the O/H/W unit, completing the seam between E and O.
- Sew the M/G/X/border-section unit to the L rectangle with a partial seam. Sew this section to the edge of the T/Y/O/P/W unit.
- Sew the top border to the edge of the A/J/T/L unit. Add the D square to the right edge.
- Complete the seam between the M/G/X/border-section unit and the L/D unit.
- Sew the left border to the edge of the N/Z/V/R unit.
- Sew the S/B unit to the top border/A/C unit.
- Complete the seam between the left border/N unit and the S/B/C unit.
- Sew the bottom border to the bottom of the quilt.

3 Stitch the socks in the lower-left corner, overlapping the toe of one sock with the top of the other.

FINISHING THE QUILT

For free, detailed instructions on finishing and other quiltmaking techniques, refer to ShopMartingale.com/HowtoQuilt.

1 Layer the quilt top, batting, and backing; baste the layers together.

2 Quilt as desired. The featured quilt is machine quilted with a variety of designs, including outline quilting around many of the T-shirt motifs, curlicues, wavy lines, and basketballs.

3 Bind with the dark-gray 2½"-wide strips. Go Zags!

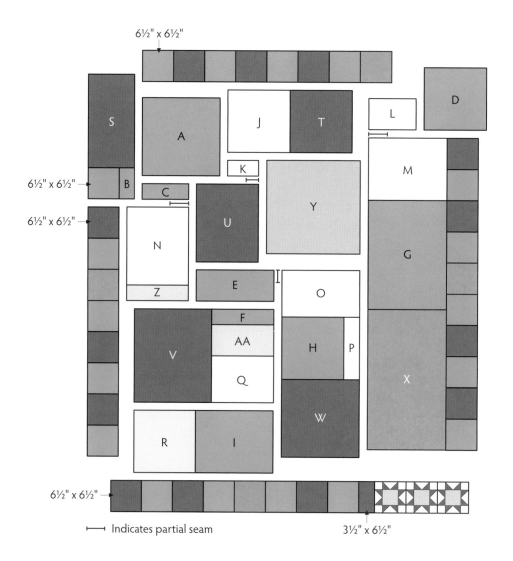

6½" x 6½"

6½" x 6½"

6½" x 6½"

6½" x 6½"

⊢━┥ Indicates partial seam

3½" x 6½"

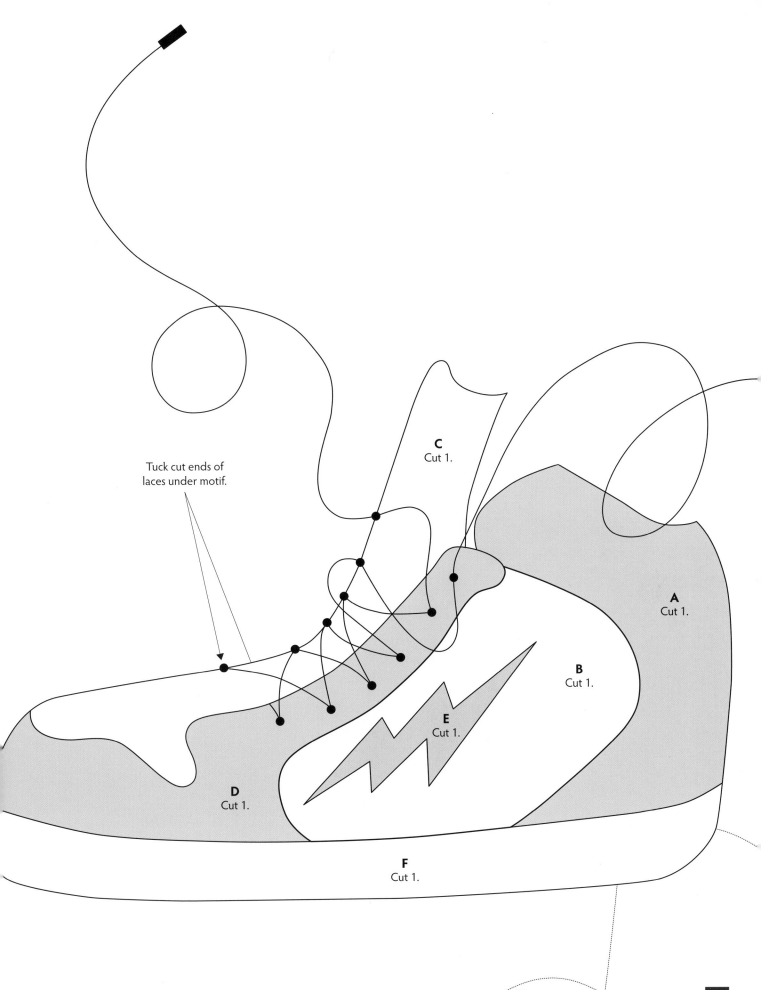

Tuck cut ends of
laces under motif.

C
Cut 1.

A
Cut 1.

B
Cut 1.

E
Cut 1.

D
Cut 1.

F
Cut 1.

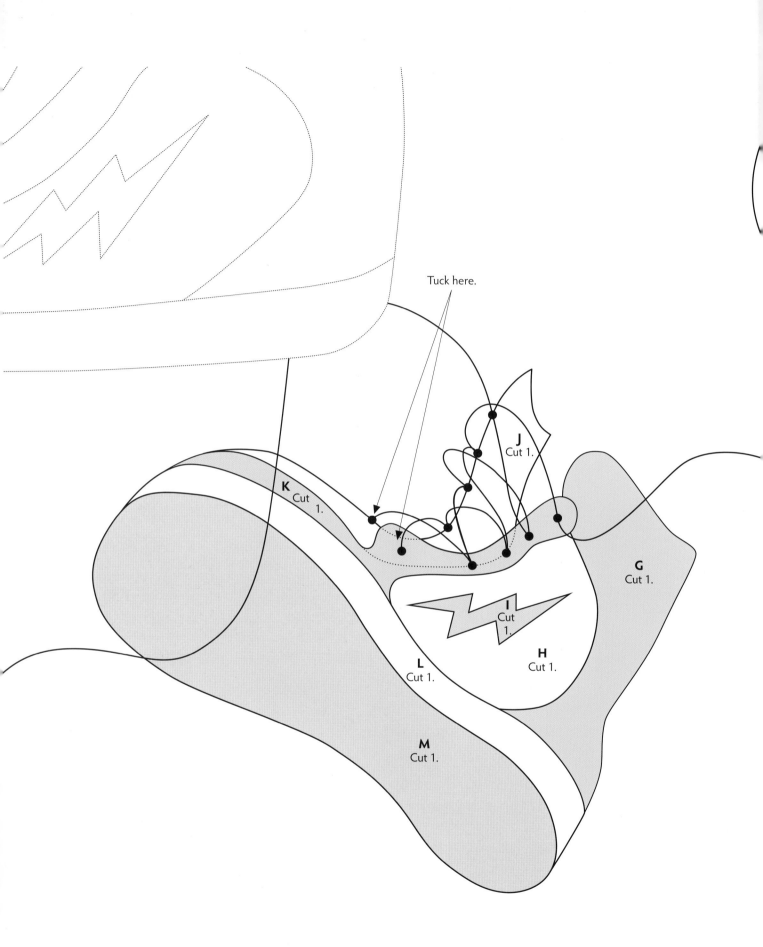

Tuck here.

J
Cut 1.

K
Cut 1.

G
Cut 1.

I
Cut 1.

H
Cut 1.

L
Cut 1.

M
Cut 1.

Winning Combination

Designed and made by Jamie Mueller
Quilt size: 67½" x 82½"

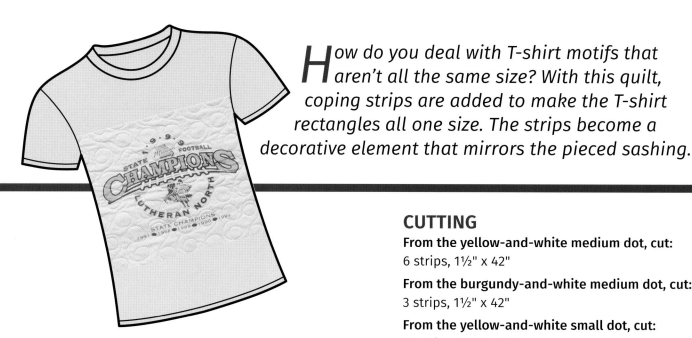

How do you deal with T-shirt motifs that aren't all the same size? With this quilt, coping strips are added to make the T-shirt rectangles all one size. The strips become a decorative element that mirrors the pieced sashing.

MATERIALS

Unless otherwise specified, yardage is based on 42"-wide fabric.

9 or more adult-sized T-shirts

1⅜ yards of burgundy solid for border

⅞ yard of dark-gray solid for sashing and cornerstones

⅝ yard of yellow-and-white small dot for sashing

⅝ yard of burgundy-and-white small dot for sashing

⅓ yard of yellow-and-white medium dot for coping strips (optional)*

¼ yard of burgundy-and-white medium dot for coping strips (optional)*

⅔ yard of cheddar solid for binding

5 yards of fabric for backing

74" x 89" piece of batting

5½ yards of 20"-wide lightweight fusible interfacing; Jamie prefers Heat N Bond featherweight

If your T-shirt pieces don't all measure 15½" x 20½", use this fabric to make coping strips. Jamie did so in five of the blocks pictured.

CUTTING

From the yellow-and-white medium dot, cut:
6 strips, 1½" x 42"

From the burgundy-and-white medium dot, cut:
3 strips, 1½" x 42"

From the yellow-and-white small dot, cut:
12 strips, 1½" x 42"

From the burgundy-and-white small dot, cut:
12 strips, 1½" x 42"

From the dark-gray solid, cut:
2 strips, 3½" x 42"; cut into 16 squares, 3½" x 3½"
12 strips, 1½" x 42"

From the burgundy solid, cut:
8 strips, 5½" x 42"

From the cheddar solid, cut:
8 strips, 2½" x 42"

PREPARING THE T-SHIRTS

1 Referring to "Stabilizing a T-Shirt" on page 6, prepare the printed front or back of each shirt with interfacing.

2 Choose one of the following options to make your T-shirt pieces all the same size.

Option 1: Trim the prepared T-shirt pieces to nine rectangles, 15½" x 20½". If necessary, piece together two shirts to get the required size. (Jamie did this in three of her blocks.)

Option 2: On five of the blocks, Jamie added pieced coping strips to get the necessary size. If you're adding the pieced coping strips, cut your prepared T-shirt pieces to the following sizes instead:

- 4 rectangles, 15½" x 20½"
- 4 rectangles, 15½" x 17½"
- 1 rectangle, 15½" x 14½"

ADDING COPING STRIPS TO T-SHIRTS (OPTIONAL)

If you selected "Option 2" and are adding the optional coping strips, follow these instructions. Otherwise, skip ahead to "Preparing the Sashing" at right.

1 Aligning the long edges, join two yellow-and-white medium dot 1½" x 42" strips and one burgundy-and-white medium dot 1½" x 42" strip to make a strip set. Press the seam allowances toward the burgundy. Repeat to make three strip sets. Cut the strip sets into six coping strips, 3½" x 15½".

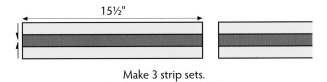

Make 3 strip sets.
Cut 6 coping strips, 15½".

2 Referring to the top-left block in the quilt layout diagram on page 36, sew a coping strip to the bottom edge of a T-shirt 15½" x 17½" rectangle. Press the seam allowances toward the coping strip. The T-shirt piece should now measure 15½" x 20½". Repeat with a second T-shirt 15½" x 17½" rectangle.

3 Adding the coping strip to the top edge instead, repeat step 2 to add coping strips to the remaining two 15½" x 17½" T-shirt rectangles.

4 Referring to the center block in the quilt layout diagram, sew coping strips to the top *and* bottom edges of the T-shirt 15½" x 14½" rectangle. Press the seam allowances toward the coping strips. The T-shirt piece should now measure 15½" x 20½".

PREPARING THE SASHING

1 Aligning the long edges and using the 1½" x 42" strips, sew a yellow-and-white small dot strip, a burgundy-and-white small dot strip, and a dark-gray solid strip as shown to make a strip set. Press the seam allowances toward the center dark-gray solid. Repeat to make 12 strip sets.

2 Cut the strip sets to make 12 pieced sashing strips, 3½" x 20½", and 12 pieced sashing strips, 3½" x 15½".

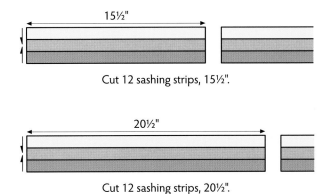

Cut 12 sashing strips, 15½".

Cut 12 sashing strips, 20½".

ASSEMBLING THE QUILT TOP

1 Referring to the quilt layout diagram on page 36, lay out T-shirt rectangles, pieced sashing strips, and dark-gray 3½" squares in seven horizontal rows. Note the placement of the burgundy and yellow fabrics when laying out the pieced sashing strips in each row.

2 Sew the pieces in each row together. Press the seam allowances toward the pieced sashing strips.

3 Join the rows and press the seam allowances toward the sashing rows.

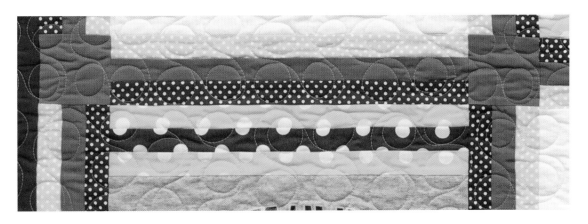

ADDING THE BORDER

1 Sew together the short ends of two burgundy 5½" x 42" strips and press the seam allowances in one direction. Repeat to make four.

2 Measure the length of the quilt through the center and cut two strips to that measurement. Sew the trimmed border strips to the long edges of quilt. Press the seam allowances toward the border.

3 Measure the width of the quilt (including the side borders) through the center and cut the remaining two strips to that measurement. Sew the trimmed border strips to the top and bottom of quilt. Press the seam allowances toward the border.

FINISHING THE QUILT

For free, detailed instructions on finishing and other quiltmaking techniques, refer to ShopMartingale.com/HowtoQuilt.

1 Layer the quilt top, batting, and backing; baste the layers together.

2 Quilt as desired. The featured quilt is machine quilted with an allover loop design.

3 Bind with the cheddar 2½"-wide strips.

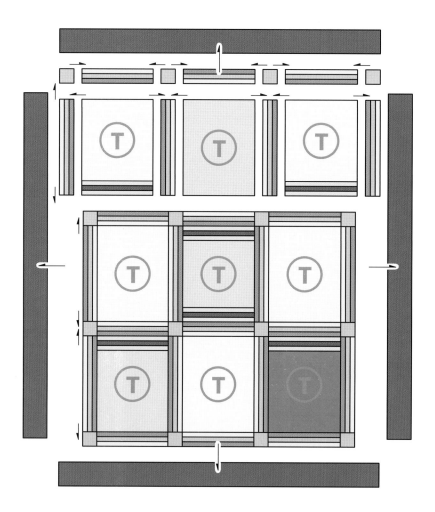

Congrats, Grad!

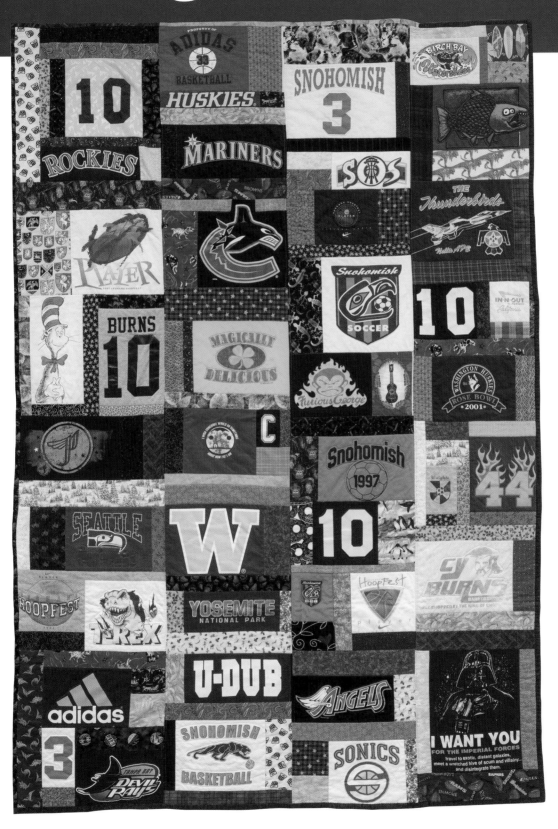

Designed and made by Mary J. Burns
Quilt size: 67¾" x 100"

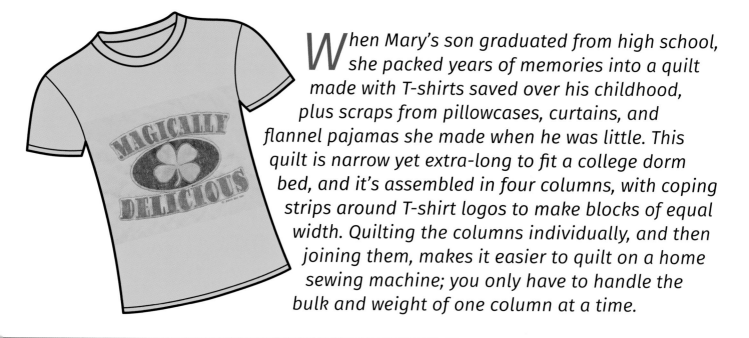

When Mary's son graduated from high school, she packed years of memories into a quilt made with T-shirts saved over his childhood, plus scraps from pillowcases, curtains, and flannel pajamas she made when he was little. This quilt is narrow yet extra-long to fit a college dorm bed, and it's assembled in four columns, with coping strips around T-shirt logos to make blocks of equal width. Quilting the columns individually, and then joining them, makes it easier to quilt on a home sewing machine; you only have to handle the bulk and weight of one column at a time.

MATERIALS

Unless otherwise specified, yardage is based on 42"-wide fabric. Rather than use the ¼" seam allowance typically used for quilting, designer Mary Burns used a ½" seam allowance because the knit edges of the T-shirts tend to roll up less with a wide seam allowance.

Approximately 44 T-shirts (if you have some shirts that are printed front and back, you may need fewer shirts)

4⅓ yards *total* of assorted prints for block borders

8 to 10 yards of 20"-wide lightweight fusible interfacing

¾ yard of brown print for binding

7⅝ yards of flannel for backing; piece and cut to make 3 pieces, 20" x 105", and 1 piece, 23" x 105"

84" x 107" piece of lightweight batting; cut into 3 pieces, 20" x 105", and 1 piece, 23" x 105"

CUTTING

From the brown print, cut:
9 strips, 2½" x 42"

PREPARING THE T-SHIRTS

Referring to "Stabilizing a T-Shirt" on page 6, prepare the front and/or back of each shirt with interfacing. When you cut your logos out, Mary recommends cutting them into rectangles or squares that are as large as possible—you can always cut them smaller to fit the size needed.

TIP — Too many logos?

If your shirts have big logos on the back and small logos on the front, you can use both sizes. Mary used a couple small logos in this quilt. There are several square pieces in this layout that could easily be replaced by small logos with a little planning.

CUTTING THE T-SHIRTS

From the printed areas of the prepared T-shirts, cut the following squares and rectangles. The dimensions that follow are for duplicating Mary's quilt (and are assigned letters A–D for the four columns). If your motif is directional, check the illustrations on pages 40–44 before you cut to make sure it will be oriented correctly in the assembled quilt. If your T-shirt logos are not these exact sizes, just adjust the surrounding strips to make blocks of the appropriate size.

Column A

A1: 11" x 11" square

A2: 13½" x 5¾" rectangle

A3: 12¾" x 11¼" rectangle

A4: 8" x 15" rectangle

A5: 9¼" x 15¼" rectangle

A6: 14" x 9¼" rectangle

A7: 12" x 9" rectangle

A8: 9½" x 9" rectangle

A9: 11¼" x 9¾" rectangle

A10: 12" x 9" rectangle

A11: 5¼" x 8½" rectangle

A12: 12½" x 8" rectangle

Column B

B1: 12½" x 9½" rectangle

B2: 14" x 3" rectangle

B3: 15" x 8" rectangle

B4: 12½" x 11" rectangle

B5: 13½" x 10½" rectangle

B6: 10½" x 9½" rectangle

B7: 4" x 6" rectangle

B8: 13½" x 10" rectangle

B9: 13¼" x 6" rectangle

B10: 14½" x 7" rectangle

B11: 12½" x 10¼" rectangle

Column C

C1: 15" x 10½" rectangle

C2: 11½" x 5¾" rectangle

C3: 9" x 8" rectangle

C4: 12½" x 13¼" rectangle

C5: 11½" x 9" rectangle

C6: 13½" x 9¼" rectangle

C7: 9¼" x 9" rectangle

C8: 6½" x 7½" rectangle

C9: 9½" x 8¾" rectangle

C10: 14" x 7" rectangle

C11: 11" x 9" rectangle

Column D

D1: 10" x 7" rectangle

D2: 14" x 9½" rectangle

D3: 15" x 11" rectangle

D4: 9¼" x 8½" rectangle

D5: 6" x 6½" rectangle

D6: 12" x 9¼" rectangle

D7: 5" x 7½" rectangle

D8: 10" x 10¼" rectangle

D9: 13½" x 10" rectangle

D10: 12½" x 17" rectangle

CUTTING AND PIECING COLUMN A

Cut the following pieces from the assorted prints and remaining T-shirts. Then use the illustration at right as a guide to piece the A column using these pieces and the T-shirt pieces cut previously. For ease of piecing, the illustration shows the column divided into blocks. Piece the blocks first, and then join the blocks to make the column. Stitch all pieces using a ½" seam allowance.

For block A1/A2:
2 rectangles, 3" x 16½"
2 rectangles, 3" x 11"
1 rectangle, 2½" x 11"
1 rectangle, 4¼" x 21"
1 rectangle, 2¼" x 16½"
1 rectangle, 4" x 5¾"

For block A3:
1 rectangle, 4¾" x 19¾"
1 rectangle, 8" x 11¼"

For block A4/A5:
1 rectangle, 2½" x 16½"
1 rectangle, 3" x 16½"
1 rectangle, 2½" x 8"
1 rectangle, 2¼" x 9¼"

For block A6/A7:
1 rectangle, 4" x 9¼"
1 rectangle, 3¾" x 9¼"
1 rectangle, 4¼" x 19¾"
1 rectangle, 2½" x 9"
1 rectangle, 5½" x 9"
1 rectangle, 2¾" x 9"

For block A8/A9:
1 rectangle, 3" x 9½"
1 rectangle, 2¼" x 11¼"

For block A10/A11/A12:
1 rectangle, 3" x 16¾"
1 rectangle, 4¼" x 5¾"
1 square, 5¾" x 5¾"
1 rectangle, 4" x 21"
1 rectangle, 4" x 12½"
1 rectangle, 3½" x 5¼"

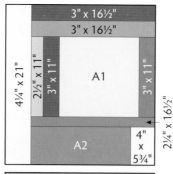
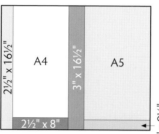
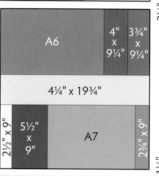
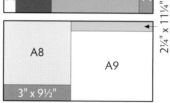
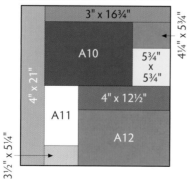

Column A assembly

Column A

CUTTING AND PIECING COLUMN B

Cut the following pieces from the assorted prints and remaining T-shirts; then follow the illustration at right to piece the B column. Stitch all pieces using a ½" seam allowance.

For block B1/B2:
1 rectangle, 5½" x 9½"
1 rectangle, 3" x 4"
1 rectangle, 3" x 17"

For block B3:
1 rectangle, 3" x 8"
1 rectangle, 3½" x 17"

For block B4:
1 rectangle, 2½" x 17"
1 rectangle, 5½" x 11"

For block B5:
1 rectangle, 5" x 17"
1 rectangle, 3¼" x 10½"
1 rectangle, 2¼" x 10½"
1 rectangle, 3" x 17"

For block B6/B7:
1 rectangle, 2" x 6"
1 rectangle, 4½" x 5"
1 rectangle, 3½" x 9½"
1 rectangle, 2¼" x 17"

For block B8:
1 rectangle, 3½" x 17"
1 rectangle, 4½" x 10"

For block B9:
1 rectangle, 3" x 17"
1 rectangle, 3¼" x 6"
1 rectangle, 2½" x 6"
1 rectangle, 3¾" x 17"

For block B10:
1 rectangle, 3½" x 7"
1 rectangle, 3" x 17"

For block B11:
1 rectangle, 2½" x 10¼"
1 rectangle, 4" x 10¼"
1 rectangle, 2¾" x 17"

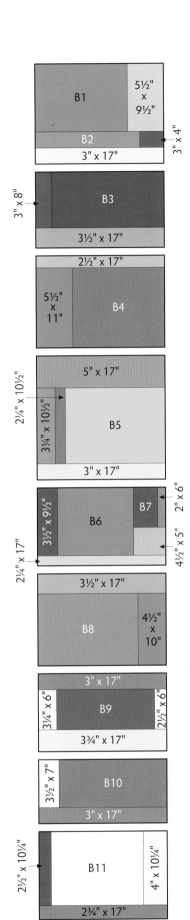

Column B assembly

Column B

CUTTING AND PIECING COLUMN C

Cut the following pieces from the assorted prints and remaining T-shirts; then follow the illustration at right to piece the C column. Stitch all pieces using a ½" seam allowance.

For block C1:
1 rectangle, 6" x 17"
1 rectangle, 3" x 10½"

For block C2/C3:
1 rectangle, 2¾" x 17"
1 rectangle, 3¼" x 6½"
1 rectangle, 3½" x 6½"
1 rectangle, 4¾" x 8"
1 rectangle, 5¼" x 8"
1 rectangle, 2½" x 17"

For block C4:
1 rectangle, 5½" x 13¼"

For block C5:
1 rectangle, 6½" x 9"
1 rectangle, 3¾" x 17"

For block C6/C7:
1 rectangle, 4½" x 9¼"
1 rectangle, 4" x 9"
1 rectangle, 5¾" x 9"

For block C8/C9:
1 rectangle, 2" x 17"
1 rectangle, 3" x 11"
1 rectangle, 4½" x 6½"
1 rectangle, 3¼" x 9½"
1 rectangle, 4" x 17"

For block C10/C11:
1 rectangle, 4" x 7"
1 rectangle, 3¼" x 17"
1 rectangle, 2½" x 9"
1 square, 5½" x 5½"
1 rectangle, 4½" x 5½"

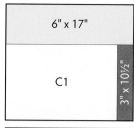

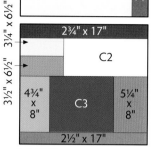

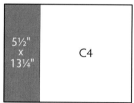

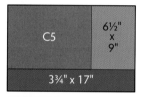

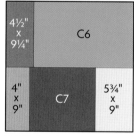

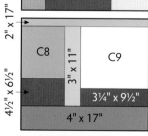

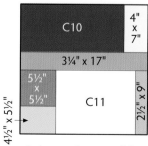

Column C assembly

Column C

CUTTING AND PIECING COLUMN D

Cut the following pieces from the assorted prints and remaining T-shirts; then follow the illustration at right to piece the D column. Stitch all pieces using a ½" seam allowance.

For block D1:
1 rectangle, 2½" x 11"
1 rectangle, 2" x 7"
1 rectangle, 5¾" x 7"
1 rectangle, 3¾" x 7"

For block D2:
1 rectangle, 4" x 13"
1 rectangle, 4½" x 14"

For block D3:
1 rectangle, 4" x 15"
1 rectangle, 3" x 14"

For block D4/D5:
1 rectangle, 3" x 6"
1 rectangle, 2¾" x 8½"
1 rectangle, 2" x 8½"
1 rectangle, 3" x 17"

For block D6:
2 rectangles, 3½" x 9¼"

For block D7/D8:
1 rectangle, 3½" x 6½"
1 rectangle, 3" x 10"
1 rectangle, 4" x 6½"
1 rectangle, 2½" x 14"
1 rectangle, 2" x 5"
1 rectangle, 2½" x 8½"
1 rectangle, 2¾" x 10"
1 rectangle, 3" x 17"

For block D9:
2 rectangles, 3½" x 17"
1 rectangle, 4½" x 10"

For block D10:
1 rectangle, 2¾" x 17"
1 rectangle, 3¾" x 17"
1 rectangle, 4¾" x 17"

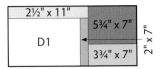

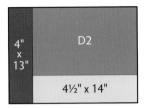

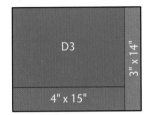

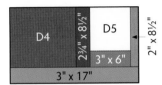

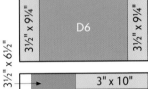

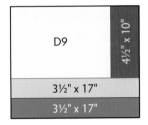

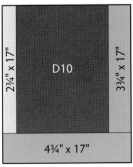

Column D assembly

Column D

QUILTING AND JOINING THE COLUMNS

1 Lay the backing 23" x 105" piece wrong side up and place the batting 23" x 105" piece on top. Center quilt-top column A, right side up, on the batting/backing; the batting/backing should extend 2" to 3" on all sides of the column. Pin baste generously; avoid placing pins where you'll quilt. Using the backing and batting 20" x 105" pieces, repeat to baste quilt-top columns B, C, and D. Quilt one column at a time, avoiding quilting in the outer ½" of the quilt-top column. Follow the logos by outlining them or create your own quilt design. Mary quilted in the ditch of many pieces and outline quilted around the T-shirt motifs.

2 Align the long edges of two adjacent columns. Pinning just the quilt-top edges, pin the long edges of the columns together, leaving the backing and batting loose (or pinned out of the way). To reduce bulk, trim only the batting (not the backing) until the two sides just meet in the middle but won't be sewn in the seam allowance. Sew the fronts together with a ½" seam allowance. Repeat to join the remaining columns.

3 Lay the joined four columns with the backing side up. Trim the long edge of the first column's backing so it ends right at the seam of the quilt top (even with the trimmed edge of the batting). Trim the long edge of the adjacent column's backing so it extends 1" past the seam of the quilt top; fold the edge under ½" and press. Overlap the raw edge of the first column with the folded backing and slip-stitch by hand just through the backing. Repeat to join the remaining columns.

4 Trim the batting and backing even with the quilt top on the outer edges of the joined columns.

BINDING THE EDGES

Bind with the brown 2½"-wide strips. For free, detailed instructions on binding and other quiltmaking techniques, refer to ShopMartingale.com/HowtoQuilt.

Designed and pieced by Andy Knowlton; quilted by Melissa Kelly
Quilt size: 50" x 56"

A simple yet striking design makes nine travel tees appear to float over a gridded background.

MATERIALS

Unless otherwise specified, yardage is based on 42"-wide fabric.

9 travel-themed T-shirts

1 yard of white solid for background and border

⅜ yard of gray solid for background

½ yard of navy solid for binding

3⅛ yards of fabric for backing

56" x 62" piece of batting

3⅞ yards of 20"-wide lightweight fusible interfacing

CUTTING

From the white solid, cut:

1 strip, 5½" x 42"; crosscut into 3 rectangles, 5½" x 11"

1 strip, 5½" x 42"; crosscut into 9 rectangles, 4¼" x 5½"

1 strip, 5½" x 42"; crosscut into:
  1 rectangle, 5½" x 11"
  3 rectangles, 4¼" x 5½"
  4 rectangles, 3¼" x 5½"

6 strips, 3" x 42"

From the gray solid, cut:

2 strips, 5½" x 42"; crosscut into 12 rectangles, 5½" x 6½"

From the navy solid, cut:

6 strips, 2½" x 42"

PREPARING THE T-SHIRTS

1 Referring to "Stabilizing a T-Shirt" on page 6, prepare the printed front or back of each shirt with interfacing.

2 Trim the prepared T-shirt pieces to 12" x 14", ensuring that the graphic is centered and level with the cut edge.

MAKING THE SASHING UNITS

Sew white 4¼" x 5½" rectangles to the 5½" edges of a gray 5½" x 6½" rectangle to make a sashing unit. Press the seam allowances toward the gray rectangle. The sashing unit should measure 5½" x 14". Repeat to make six sashing units.

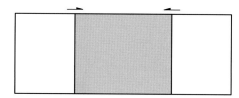

Make 6.

Picture Perfect

TIP

This neutral quilt lends itself to many different looks, especially with the addition of cotton prints. Spice up the design by using a novelty print suitable to the theme of the T-shirts in the solid gray or white areas. Or use 4" x 6" photos from the trips or activities depicted in the T-shirts; print them onto printable fabric sheets and use those in the solid gray areas.

ASSEMBLING THE QUILT TOP

1 Arrange the T-shirt rectangles, sashing units, white 3¼" x 5½" rectangles, gray 5½" x 6½" rectangles, and white 5½" x 11" rectangles in five rows as shown.

2 Sew together the pieces in each row. In the T-shirt rows, press the seam allowances toward the T-shirt rectangles. In the remaining rows, press the seam allowances toward the gray rectangles.

3 Join the rows to make the quilt center. Press the seam allowances toward the pieced sashing rows.

4 Remove the selvages from the white 3" x 42" strips. Sew the strips end to end to make one strip.

5 Measure the length of the quilt top through the center of the quilt. Cut two border strips to that length. Sew the border strips to the sides of the quilt. Press the seam allowances toward the borders.

6 Measure the width of the quilt top through the center of the quilt, including the just-added borders. Cut two border strips to that length. Sew the borders to the top and bottom of the quilt top. Press the seam allowances toward the borders.

FINISHING THE QUILT

For free, detailed instructions on finishing and other quiltmaking techniques, refer to ShopMartingale.com/HowtoQuilt.

1 Layer the quilt top, batting, and backing; baste the layers together.

2 Quilt as desired. The featured quilt is machine quilted with an allover square spiral design.

3 Bind with the navy 2½"-wide strips.

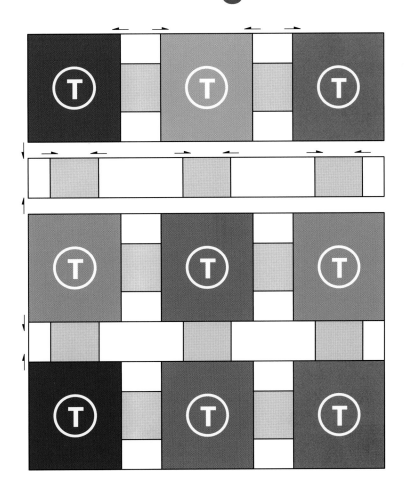

Tween Dreams

Designed and pieced by Sheila Markewicz; quilted by Richla Ramsey
Quilt size: 66½" x 80½"

It started with some old T-shirts that Sheila's daughter had outgrown. The images on the shirts ranged in size from small 5" or 6" designs up to 16" to 18". Sheila envisioned a collage or scrapbook-style layout, so she began by arranging the T-shirts on the floor and moving them around until she was happy with the placement. Because T-shirts and jeans go together like peanut butter and jelly (or teenagers and cell phones), she wanted to incorporate the look of jeans. To avoid the weight and bulk of actual denim, she opted for cotton prints in shades of denim blue. Colorful prints frame each T-shirt, lightening the look of the quilt.

MATERIALS

Unless otherwise specified, yardage is based on 42"-wide fabric. Fat quarters are 18" x 21".

18 T-shirts

18 fat quarters of assorted prints for T-shirt borders and sashing

13 fat quarters of assorted denim-blue prints for sashing

⅝ yard of light-gray print for binding

5 yards of fabric for backing

74" x 88" piece of batting

5 yards of 20"-wide lightweight fusible interfacing; Sheila prefers 911FF Pellon Fusible Featherweight

PREPARING THE T-SHIRTS

1 Cut apart each T-shirt to preserve the maximum surface area to be stabilized. For smaller T-shirts this may mean cutting down the back and across the top of the sleeves. A small portion of a sleeve or neck seam may end up in the seam allowance of the cut T-shirt. Cut apart larger T-shirts along the sides and up through the sleeves. Cut a piece of interfacing about 2" larger than the dimensions you want to cut each T-shirt.

2 Referring to "Stabilizing a T-Shirt" on page 6, prepare the printed front or back of each shirt with interfacing.

CUTTING

The first measurement in each case is width because all of these are directional. Because the border strips are oversized and the finished block will be trimmed, don't worry if your T-shirt rectangles and squares are a little larger or smaller than the list below.

From the assorted prepared T-shirts, cut:

1 rectangle, 13½" x 9½", for block E1

1 rectangle, 12½" x 4½", for block C3

1 square, 12" x 12", for block F2

1 rectangle, 11½" x 17", for block A

1 rectangle, 11½" x 16½", for block G2

1 rectangle, 11½" x 15½", for block B

1 square, 11½" x 11½", for block E2

1 square, 10½" x 10½", for block D3

1 rectangle, 10" x 13½", for block H1

1 rectangle, 10" x 13", for block I2

1 rectangle, 10" x 12½", for block D1

1 rectangle, 9½" x 10½", for block H2

1 square, 9½" x 9½", for block C2

1 rectangle, 9" x 7", for block F1

1 square, 7½" x 7½", for block G1

1 square, 7" x 7", for block C1

1 square, 6½" x 6½", for block D2

1 square, 5" x 5", for block I1

From *each of 14* of the assorted prints, cut:

4 strips, 2½" x 21"

Continued on page 50

Continued from page 49

From *each* of the remaining 4 prints, cut:
4 strips, 3½" x 21"

From the assorted denim-blue prints, cut:
85 strips, 2½" x 21"

From the light-gray print, cut:
8 strips, 2½" x 42"

MAKING THE BLOCKS

1 Sew matching 3½" x 21" strips to the sides of the T-shirt 13½" x 9½" rectangle. Press the seam allowances toward the strips; trim the strips even with the T-shirt rectangle. Add matching 3½" x 21" strips to the top and bottom. Press as before. Trim to 18½" x 14½" to make block E1.

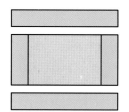
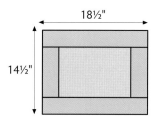

18½"

14½"

2 Repeat step 1 to sew 3½" x 21" strips to each rectangle or square listed below, and then trim to the indicated size.

- 1 square, 12" x 12"; trim to 16½" x 16½" to make block F2
- 1 rectangle, 9½" x 10½"; trim to 12½" x 14½" to make block H2
- 1 square, 5" x 5"; trim to 10½" x 10½" to make block I1

3 Sew matching 2½" x 21" strips to the sides of the T-shirt 11½" x 17" rectangle. Press the seam allowances toward the strips; trim the strips even with the T-shirt rectangle. Add matching 2½" x 21" strips to the top and bottom. Press as before. Trim to 14½" x 20½" to make block A.

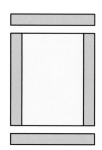
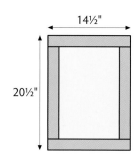

14½"

20½"

4 Repeat step 3 to sew 2½" x 21" strips to each rectangle or square listed below, and then trim to the indicated size.

- 1 rectangle, 12½" x 4½"; trim to 14½" x 6½" to make block C3
- 1 rectangle, 11½" x 16½"; trim to 14½" x 18½" to make block G2
- 1 rectangle, 11½" x 15½"; trim to 14½" x 18½" to make block B
- 1 square, 11½" x 11½"; trim to 14½" x 14½" to make block E2
- 1 square, 10½" x 10½"; trim to 12½" x 12½" to make block D3
- 1 rectangle, 10" x 13½"; trim to 12½" x 16½" to make block H1
- 1 rectangle, 10" x 13"; trim to 12½" x 16½" to make block I2
- 1 rectangle, 10" x 12½"; trim to 12½" x 14½" to make block D1
- 1 square, 9½" x 9½"; trim to 12½" x 12½" to make block C2
- 1 rectangle, 9" x 7"; trim to 12½" x 10½" to make block F1
- 1 square, 7½" x 7½"; trim to 10½" x 10½" to make block G1
- 1 square, 7" x 7"; trim to 10½" x 10½" to make block C1
- 1 square, 6½" x 6½"; trim to 8½" x 8½" to make block D2

MAKING THE SASHING

1 Sew together five denim-blue strips along their long edges to make a strip set. Press the seam allowances in one direction. Repeat to make 17 strip sets.

2 Cut the strip sets into 119 blue sashing segments, each 2½" wide.

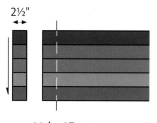

2½"

Make 17 strip sets.
Cut 7 segments from each.

3 From the leftover assorted 3½" x 21" and 2½" x 21" strips, cut 60 squares, 2½" x 2½".

4 Join five assorted squares to make a multicolored sashing segment. Press the seam allowances in one direction. Repeat to make the following multicolored sashing segments.

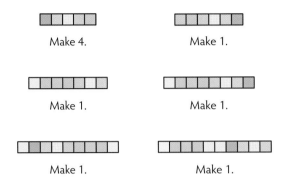

Make 4.

Make 1.

Make 1.

Make 1.

Make 1.

Make 1.

ASSEMBLING THE QUILT TOP

1 Referring to the quilt layout diagram below, lay out the blue sashing segments, the multicolored sashing segments, and the T-shirt pieces for each of sections A–I. You may need to shorten some sashing segments by removing squares, or you may need to add one or two squares to lengthen a segment.

2 Sew the pieces in each section together. To make it easiest to join the sashing segments, the seam allowances of adjacent segments should be pressed in opposite directions; this may mean re-pressing the seam allowances on some of the segments.

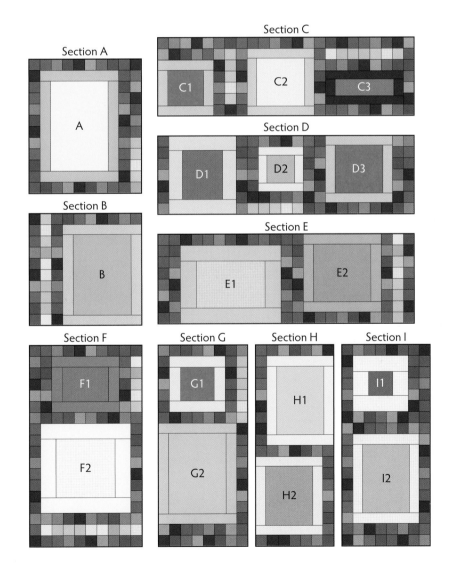

3 Sew sections A and B together. Join sections C, D, and E. Sew A/B to C/D/E.

4 Sew sections F, G, H, and I together. Add this to the bottom edge of the first unit to complete the quilt top.

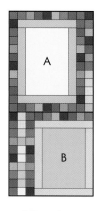

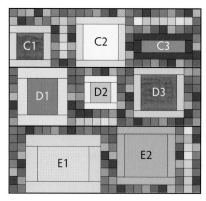

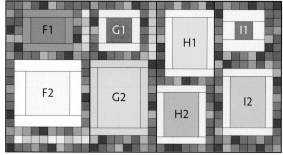

FINISHING THE QUILT

For free, detailed instructions on finishing and other quiltmaking techniques, refer to ShopMartingale.com/HowtoQuilt.

1 Layer the quilt top, batting, and backing; baste the layers together.

2 Quilt as desired. The featured quilt is machine quilted with an overall design of flowers and swirls.

3 Bind with the light-gray 2½"-wide strips.

TIP — Planning a Quilt

The instructions on pages 48–52 are for duplicating designer Sheila Markewicz's quilt. If you'd like to plan your own quilt, cut T-shirt squares and rectangles to whatever size fits your shirts best. Add a border to each T-shirt square or rectangle to make each piece a size that's divisible by 2 plus ½" for the seam allowance, such as 6½" x 8½" or 12½" x 14½".

Using graph paper with each square representing a 2" square, cut out pieces of colored paper to represent the finished measurement of each T-shirt and its corresponding border. Label each with a title and the finished dimensions. Arrange on the graph paper according to the desired layout, paying special attention to placement of the T-shirt blocks to avoid partial seams. (See the illustration on page 51 for a look at Sheila's layout.) This will be your master guide for setting the blocks into the quilt. When assembling the quilt top, you will fill in the remaining areas with denim-colored sashing. Anywhere you have more than two rows of sashing, add pieced 2½" squares from the border prints instead to lighten the look.

In Tune

Designed and pieced by Andy Knowlton; quilted by Melissa Kelly
Quilt size: 53½" x 64½"

Whether the recipient's favorite pastime is music, dance, or cheer, this design—featuring easy fusible appliqué—has you covered. There are three appliqué patterns to choose from.

MATERIALS

Unless otherwise specified, yardage is based on 42"-wide fabric.

12 T-shirts

2½ yards of white solid for sashing and border

⅝ yard of red solid for sashing squares and binding

⅓ yard of black solid, yellow solid, or pink solid for appliqué (plus ⅛ yard of contrasting fabric for the letters if using the megaphone appliqué)

3⅜ yards of fabric for backing

60" x 71" piece of batting

4⅔ yards of 20"-wide lightweight fusible interfacing

⅓ yard of fusible web

CUTTING

From the white solid, cut on the *lengthwise* grain:
1 strip, 13" x 63"

From the remaining white solid, cut:
5 strips, 2½" x 42"
8 strips, 2½" x 14"
9 strips, 2½" x 12"

From the red solid, cut:
7 strips, 2½" x 42"
6 squares, 2½" x 2½"

PREPARING THE T-SHIRTS

1 Referring to "Stabilizing a T-Shirt" on page 6, prepare the printed front or back of each shirt with interfacing.

2 Trim the prepared T-shirt pieces to 12" x 14", ensuring that the graphic is centered and level with the cut edge.

ASSEMBLING THE QUILT TOP

Referring to the quilt layout diagram on the facing page, arrange the T-shirt rectangles, white sashing strips, and red sashing squares in seven rows. Sew the pieces together in each row. Press the seam allowances toward the T-shirt rectangles and the sashing squares. Join the rows; press the seam allowances toward the sashing rows.

ADDING THE APPLIQUÉ

The appliqué patterns are on pages 56–63. Choose which appliqué shape (treble clef, ballet shoes, or cheer megaphone) you'd like to use.

1 Using a pencil, trace the applique design onto the paper side of fusible web. Cut out around each shape, leaving about ¼" around the drawn line.

2 Following the manufacturer's directions, press the fusible-web shapes onto the wrong side of the desired fabric. Cut out the appliqué shape directly on the line. Remove the paper backing and discard.

3 Place the appliqué shape(s) on the white 13" x 63" strip; be sure the appliqué is about 1" from the bottom edge and at least ½" away from the remaining edges. Fuse in place following the manufacturer's instructions.

4 Stitch around the edges of the appliqué using coordinating thread and a blanket, zigzag, or straight stitch.

ADDING THE BORDERS

1 Sew the white 2½" x 42" strips end to end to make one long strip.

2 Measure the length of the quilt top through the center of the quilt. Cut one border strip to that length. Cut the appliquéd strip to the same length. Sew the borders to the long edges of the quilt. Press the seam allowances toward the borders.

3 Measure the width of the quilt top through the center of the quilt. Cut two border strips to that length. Sew the borders to the top and bottom edge of the quilt. Press the seam allowances toward the borders.

FINISHING THE QUILT

For free, detailed instructions on finishing and other quiltmaking techniques, refer to ShopMartingale.com/HowtoQuilt.

1 Layer the quilt top, batting, and backing; baste the layers together.

2 Quilt as desired. The featured quilt is machine quilted with an allover meander connected by music notes.

3 Bind with the red 2½"-wide strips.

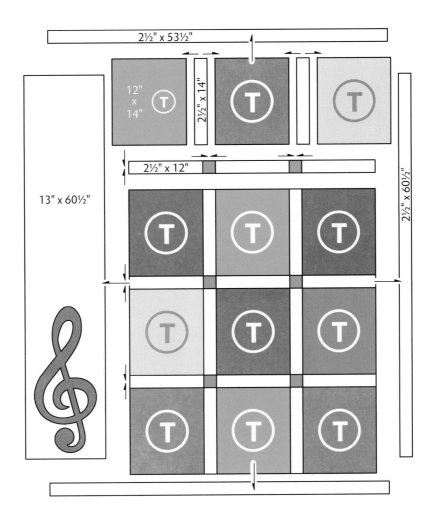

Patterns are reversed
for fusible appliqué.
Join to pattern on page 57.

Patterns are reversed
for fusible appliqué.
Join to pattern on page 56.

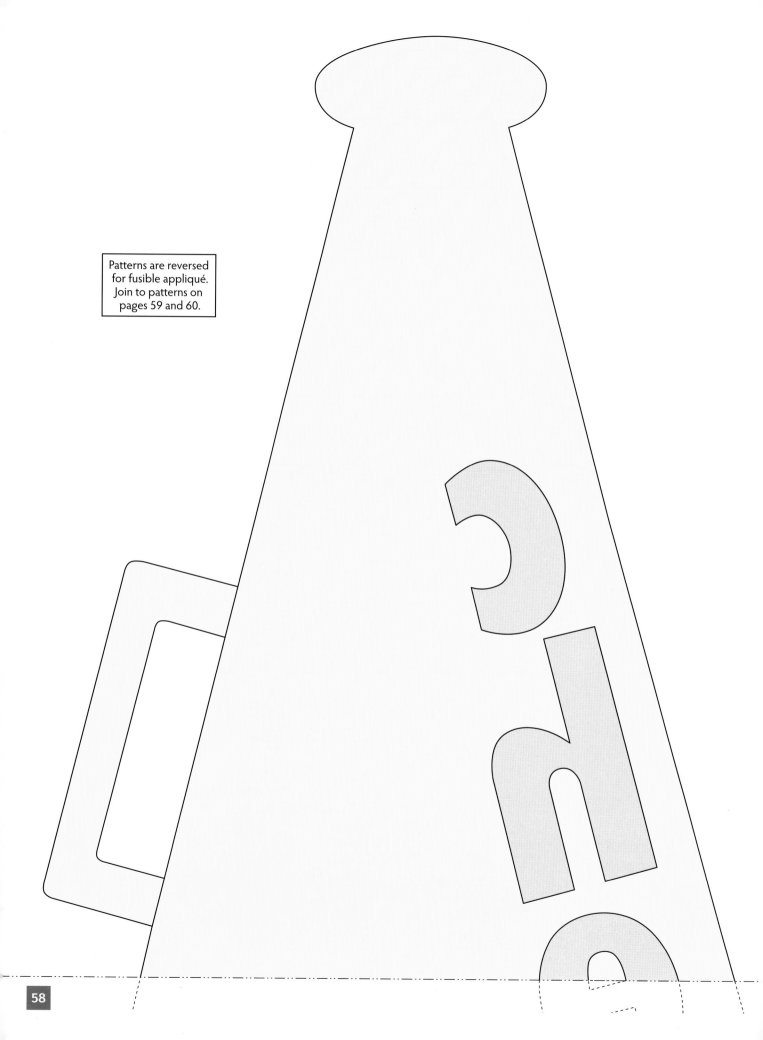

Patterns are reversed
for fusible appliqué.
Join to patterns on
pages 59 and 60.

Patterns are reversed for fusible appliqué. Join to patterns on pages 58 and 60.

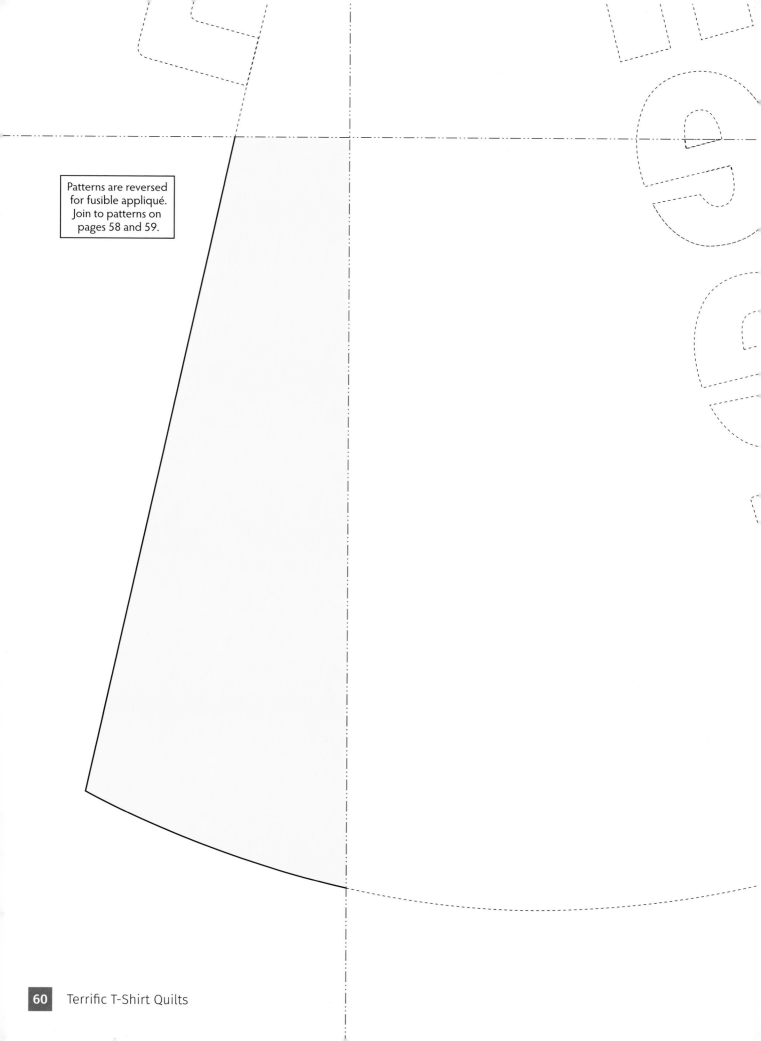

Patterns are reversed
for fusible appliqué.
Join to patterns on
pages 58 and 59.

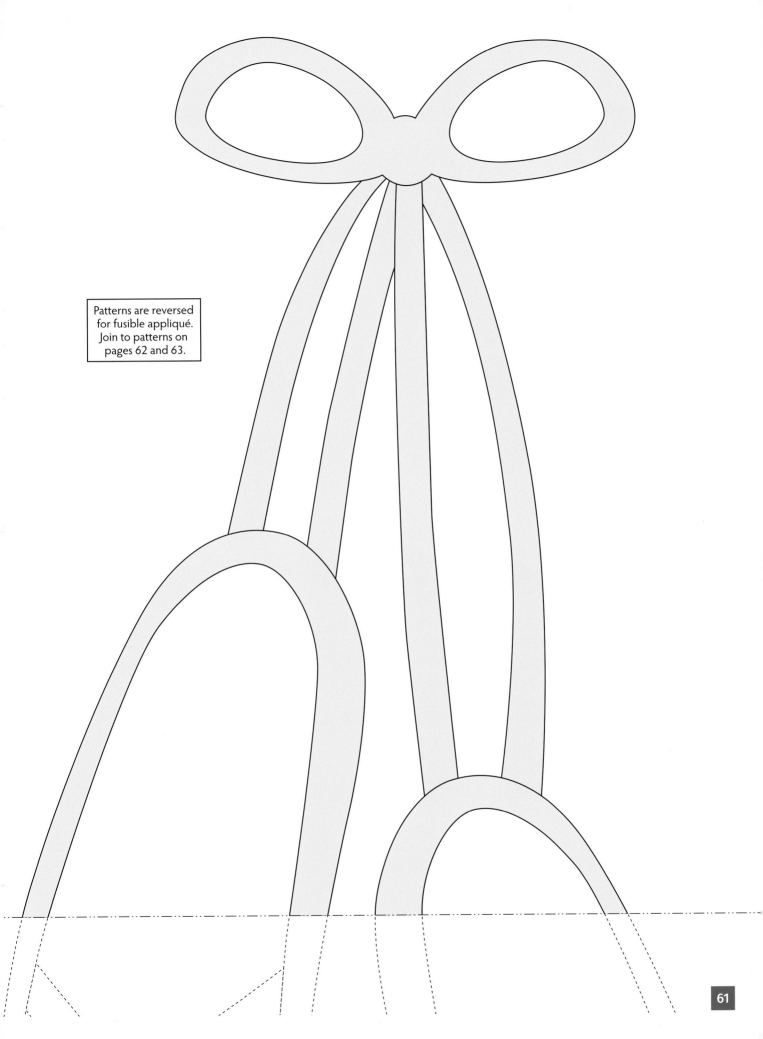

Patterns are reversed for fusible appliqué. Join to patterns on pages 62 and 63.

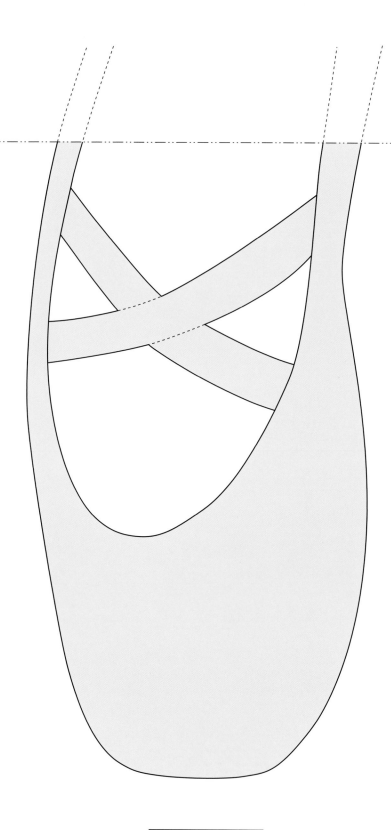

Patterns are reversed
for fusible appliqué.
Join to pattern on
page 61.

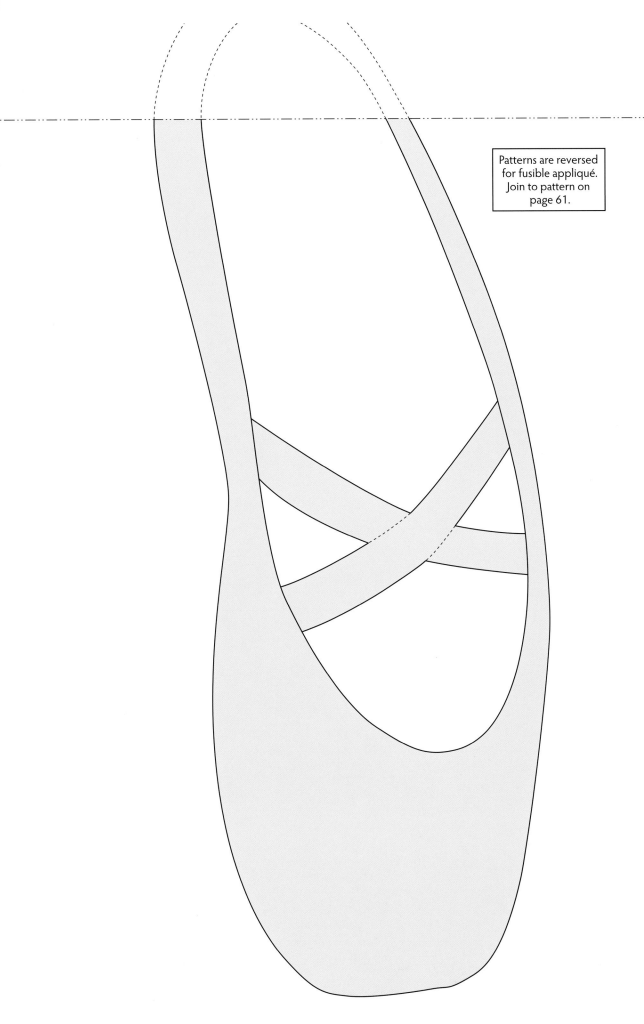

Patterns are reversed
for fusible appliqué.
Join to pattern on
page 61.

About the Contributors

PENNY BARNES

Penny, an Iowa gal, has been quilting for over 25 years. Penny turned that hobby into a business in 2013 when she opened her own long-arm studio, PB & J Quilt Studio. When not quilting for others, she loves to spend time designing her own quilts and making quilts for gifts. She and her husband enjoy traveling regularly to Ireland, occasionally even leading tours there, as well as spending time with their kids and grandkids.

ELIZABETH TISINGER BEESE

Elizabeth has been sewing for as long as she can remember, inheriting the love of sewing, crafting, and generally just "making things" from her great-grandmother Vida. Her latest T-shirt quilts include several memory quilts for her husband's family using his grandparents' clothing.

MARY J. BURNS

Mary has always been a crafty sort, and has been quilting since 1977. She also knits and crochets with sometimes hilarious results, and her latest passion is embroidery. Born incapable of not volunteering, she has also been a guild president and quilt-show chairwoman. Her designs have been published in four previous Martingale books, her photogenic dog Rufus has been in almost as many! Mary enjoys family time, gardening, antiquing, sports, movies, travel, and anything outdoors. She lives with her high-school sweetheart in their restored 1901 farmhouse in Snohomish, Washington.

ANDY KNOWLTON

Andy is a quilter and pattern designer who vividly remembers getting her first quilting lesson from Grandma when she was just seven years old. She loves to create and tries to make time each day for doing something creative, even if it's just making LEGO airplanes and crayon drawings with her kids. She's been blogging at ABrightCorner.com since 2008 and enjoys teaching and sharing her love of color, fabric, and quilting with others. Andy lives in Utah with her husband and two children, and has a great appreciation for a well-made chocolate chip cookie.

SHEILA MARKEWICZ

Sheila lives in Bothell, Washington, with her husband, two teenagers, and two dogs. They also currently have two rabbits and six chickens on their backyard "farm." She has a lifelong love of all things crafty and creative and enjoys sewing, knitting, making handmade cards, and scrapbooking. Not long before her second child was born, Sheila discovered quilting and became an avid collector of quilt patterns and fabric. In spite of having collected patterns and fabric for a number of years, she considers herself a novice quilter, having only made a half dozen or so quilts so far. The T-shirt quilt she made for this book is her first venture in designing a quilt.

KRISTA MOSER

Krista is a quilting and fiber-arts enthusiast who has taught sewing and quilting lessons for more then twenty years. She came to love the texture and dimension that machine quilting would add to any project (not just quilts!) and thus began her professional machine-quilting career at the tender age of fourteen. She now works full time teaching, designing, and most of all, adding her machine-quilted touch to her clients' projects. She is honored to have her work featured in quilting magazines, published in books, and hung in prominent quilt shops around the country.

JAMIE MUELLER

Jamie currently lives in St. Louis, Missouri, with her husband, Jonathan, and son, Jared. She spends her time quilting and sewing. Jamie's mother, Jill, taught her to sew at a very early age. After graduating from Concordia University with a Bachelor of Arts degree, her focus shifted to sewing, and she became partners with her mother at Sunflower Quilts. At Sunflower Quilts, they design patterns and notions (such as their Thread Cutter tool for chain piecing), sell custom quilts, and offer machine quilting.

JANET NESBITT

Janet is the owner of One S1ster LLC, a web-based quilt-design company and wholesaler. For the past 18 years, she has owned and operated Buggy Barn Quilts in Reardan, Washington. She also designs fabric for Henry Glass & Co. Janet has always been an avid scrap quilter with a passion for mixing prints and plaids. She especially loves creating fun and whimsical designs using her popular Crazy-piecing technique (stacking fabric, cutting on the lines, shuffling, and stitching it all together).

JACKIE WHITE

Jackie is a mother of two young boys and married to a wonderful man. Her passion is creating 3D art quilts and teaching her techniques. Jackie loves embellishing so much that half her studio is designated to embellishments! Her work has been juried into shows across North America and her patterns have been published in several books and magazines. When she's not in her studio making 3D art quilts, you can find her on Facebook at Jackie's Art Quilts.